McGRAW-HILL
THESAURUS

**McGraw-Hill
School Division**

New York   Farmington

D1347699

McGraw-Hill School Division ⊗

A Division of The McGraw·Hill Companies

Copyright © 1998 McGraw-Hill School Division, a Division
of the Educational and Professional Publishing Group of
The McGraw-Hill Companies, Inc.

McGraw-Hill School Division
1221 Avenue of the Americas
New York, New York 10020

Printed in Colombia
ISBN 0-02-244255-3
8 9 10 QWC 08 07

McGRAW-HILL
THESAURUS

How to Use the Thesaurus

Thesaurus Entry

Have you ever looked for just the right word to make a sentence more interesting or exciting? You could find that word in a thesaurus. A **thesaurus** is a collection of synonyms and antonyms. It can help you with your writing.

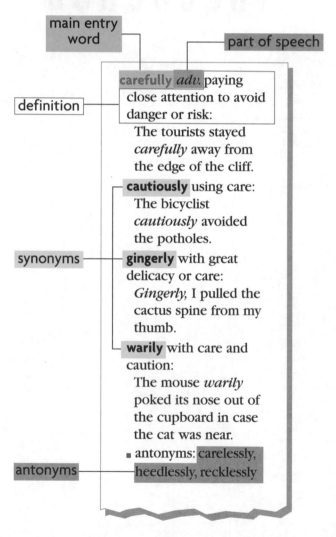

main entry word

part of speech

definition

carefully *adv.* paying close attention to avoid danger or risk:
The tourists stayed *carefully* away from the edge of the cliff.

cautiously using care:
The bicyclist *cautiously* avoided the potholes.

synonyms

gingerly with great delicacy or care:
Gingerly, I pulled the cactus spine from my thumb.

warily with care and caution:
The mouse *warily* poked its nose out of the cupboard in case the cat was near.

■ antonyms: carelessly, heedlessly, recklessly

antonyms

Thesaurus Index

The index can help you find what is in your **thesaurus**. The index is a listing of every entry word in the **thesaurus** and includes every synonym. The index also lists antonyms for selected entry words. All the words are in alphabetical order.

Each **entry word** is listed in red:

carefully *adv.*

To find this entry word, look in the **thesaurus** under **C**.

Each synonym is listed in bold black print. Next to the synonym is the synonym's entry word.

cautiously carefully *adv.*

To find the meaning of the word *cautiously*, look up the thesaurus entry for **carefully**.

Each antonym is listed in light black. Next to the antonym is the entry word.

increase **decrease** *vb.*

KEY   entry word = **bold red**   synonym = **bold black**
antonym = light black   part of speech = *italic*

n. = *noun*   *v.* or *vb.* = *verb*   *adj.* = *adjective*
adv. = *adverb*   *pl.* = *plural*   *prep.* = *preposition*

Note: A few **thesaurus** entries have so many synonyms that you'll find a box full of synonyms instead of sentences. The box may also have some antonyms.

A

angry **furious** *adj.*
annoy **bother** *vb.*
annoy **tease** *vb.*
annoy *vb.*
answer **reply** *vb.*
antiquated **modern** *adj.*
antique **modern** *adj.*
anything **nothing** *n.*
apart **alone** *adv.*
appear **disappear** *vb.*
appear **vanish** *vb.*
appear *vb.*
appoint **employ** *vb.*
appointment **date** *n.*
appreciative **grateful** *adj.*
approach **reach** *vb.*
approve **adopt** *vb.*
approve **agree** *vb.*
approve **allow** *vb.*
approved **official** *adj.*
aptitudes **abilities** *n.*
argue **fight** *vb.*
argument *n.*
argument **quarrel** *n.*
arid **damp** *adj.*
aroma **perfume** *n.*
array **variety** *n.*
arrive **leave** *vb.*
arrive **reach** *vb.*
ask **order** *vb.*

ask **reply** *vb.*
asleep **alert** *adj.*
assemble **manufacture** *vb.*
assignment **mission** *n.*
assist **hamper** *vb.*
association **club** *n.*
association **union** *n.*
assortment **variety** *n.*
assumption **notion** *n.*
assurance **promise** *n.*
astonish **amaze** *vb.*
astound **amaze** *vb.*
at once **immediately** *adv.*
attach **fasten** *vb.*
attach **join** *vb.*
attain **gain** *vb.*
attentive **alert** *adj.*
attentive **careless** *adj.*
attire **outfit** *n.*
attract **lure** *vb.*
atypical **natural** *adj.*
authorized **official** *adj.*
award **prize** *n.*
award **trophy** *n.*
away **absent** *adj.*
awful *adj.*
awful **terrible** *adj.*

KEY entry word = **bold red**   synonym = **bold black**
antonym = light black   part of speech = *italic*

B

bag *n.*
ban **permit** *vb.*
ban **require** *vb.*
bang **noise** *n.*
banquet *n.*
bar **permit** *vb.*
bar **require** *vb.*
barely *adv.*
barge **prowl** *vb.*
basic *adj.*
batch **group** *n.*
battle *n.*
be convinced **believe** *vb.*
be sure **guess** *vb.*
begin **finish** *vb.*
begin **quit** *vb.*
beginning **final** *adj.*
belief **faith** *n.*
belief **opinion** *n.*
believe *vb.*
bellow **howl** *n.*
bellow **roar** *vb.*
bellow **scream** *vb.*
beneficial **useful** *adj.*
bent *adj.*
beside **near** *prep.*
bevy **horde** *n.*
bind **fasten** *vb.*
bland **mild** *adj.*
blare **noise** *n.*

blaring **loud** *adj.*
blaring **quiet** *adj.*
blast **noise** *n.*
blast **racket** *n.*
blast **wind** *n.*
blaze **brighten** *vb.*
blaze **flare** *n.*
blaze **glare** *n.*
blissfully **happily** *adv.*
blithely **happily** *adv.*
block **neighborhood** *n.*
blunder **mistake** *n.*
boil *vb.*
boiling **angry** *adj.*
bolted **fled** *vb.*
boo **honor** *vb.*
book **novel** *n.*
boom **noise** *n.*
booming **quiet** *adj.*
boost **raise** *vb.*
border **edge** *n.*
border *n.*
bordering **nearby** *adj.*
bore **amaze** *vb.*
bore **charm** *vb.*
bored **curious** *adj.*
boring **dull** *adj.*
boring **exciting** *adj.*
boss *n.*
bother **annoy** *vb.*
bother *vb.*
bother **worry** *vb.*
bottomless **deep** *adj.*

boulder rock *n.*

bound *vb.*

boundary border *n.*

bracing exciting *adj.*

brand-new *adj.*

brave **afraid** *adj.*

bravery **fear** *n.*

brawny mighty *adj.*

breathtaking exciting *adj.*

breeze wind *n.*

bright *adj.*

bright **dark** *adj.*

bright smart *adj.*

brighten *vb.*

brightness **shadows** *n.*

brilliant bright *adj.*

bring down **raise** *vb.*

buddies friends *n.*

build create *vb.*

built *vb.*

bumpy rough *adj.*

bumpy uneven *adj.*

bunch group *n.*

bundle package *n.*

burden *n.*

burrow cave *n.*

bustle hurry *n.*

buzz noise *n.*

C

caller visitor *n.*

calm *adj.*

calm **alarm** *vb.*

calm **angry** *adj.*

calm **furious** *adj.*

calm mild *adj.*

calm **racket** *n.*

calm **scare** *vb.*

calm **worry** *vb.*

cap lid *n.*

captivate charm *vb.*

capture **give** *vb.*

careful *adj.*

carefully *adv.*

careless *adj.*

careless **careful** *adj.*

carelessly **carefully** *adv.*

carnival *n.*

carry *vb.*

casual informal *adj.*

catch **throw** *vb.*

categorize sort *v.*

category **nature** *n.*

category type *n.*

cautious **careful** *adj.*

cautiously **carefully** *adv.*

cave *n.*

cavern cave *n.*

---

competitive jealous *adj.*

complaint protest *n.*

complete finish *vb.*

completely barely *adv.*

completely quite *adv.*

comply obey *vb.*

compose create *vb.*

concealed hid *vb.*

concealed hidden *adj.*

concealed secret *adj.*

conceit pride *n.*

concern worry *vb.*

conclude finish *vb.*

conclude quit *vb.*

concluding final *adj.*

concoct maneuver *vb.*

confidence faith *n.*

confine limit *vb.*

conflict argument *n.*

conflict battle *n.*

conflict quarrel *n.*

confound amaze *vb.*

connect fasten *vb.*

connect join *vb.*

consent agree *vb.*

consequence effect *n.*

constant frequent *adj.*

constructed built *vb.*

contemporary modern *adj.*

contemporary prehistoric *adj.*

contest fight *n.*

continual frequent *adj.*

continually always *adv.*

continue finish *vb.*

continue quit *vb.*

continue remain *vb.*

continues goes *vb.*

conversation discussion *n.*

conviction opinion *n.*

cook boil *vb.*

cool cold *adj.*

copy create *vb.*

cord yarn *n.*

core center *n.*

core inside *n.*

core outside *n.*

correct exact *adj.*

correct mistaken *adj.*

correct wrong *adj.*

corridor hall *n.*

counsel advice *n.*

courage fear *n.*

course *n.*

courteous impolite *adj.*

courtesy favor *n.*

courtesy *n.*

cover lid *n.*

cover shelter *vb.*

covered hid *vb.*

covered open *adj.*

covered secret *adj.*

delay hesitate *vb.*
delicate weak *adj.*
delight bother *vb.*
delight enjoyment *noun*
delight joy *n.*
delight worry *vb.*
delightful pleasant *adj.*
delightful wonderful *adj.*
deliver provide *vb.*
demand require *vb.*
demolished built *vb.*
deny *vb.*
depart leave *vb.*
depart reach *vb.*
depart return *vb.*
depend *vb.*
depict describe *vb.*
describe *vb.*
deserve *vb.*
deserved unfair *adj.*
deserving worthy *adj.*
design create *vb.*
designed meant *vb.*
despise love *vb.*
destroy create *vb.*
destructive harmful *adj.*
detach fasten *vb.*
detailed careful *adj.*
device instrument *n.*
devise maneuver *vb.*

devotion loyalty *n.*
diary journal *n.*
different equal *adj.*
different twin *adj.*
different usual *adj.*
difficult easy *adj.*
dillydally loiter *vb.*
dim brighten *vb.*
dim dark *adj.*
diminish decrease *vb.*
diminutive tall *adj.*
dimness shadows *n.*
din noise *n.*
din racket *n.*
dinner banquet *n.*
director leader *n.*
dirt *n.*
disagree agree *vb.*
disagree fight *vb.*
disagreeable enjoyable *adj.*
disagreeable pleasant *adj.*
disagreeable wonderful *adj.*
disagreement argument *n.*
disappear appear *vb.*
disappear vanish *vb.*
disappear *vb.*
disappoint *vb.*
disapprove adopt *vb.*
discard receive *vb.*

KEY
entry word = **bold red**   synonym = **bold black**
antonym = light black   part of speech = *italic*

11

dull **bright** *adj.*
dull **brighten** *vb.*
dull **exciting** *adj.*
dull **grand** *adj.*
dull **keen** *adj.*
dull pedestrian *adj.*
dull plain *adj.*
duty chore *n.*
duty mission *n.*
dwindle decrease *vb.*

early **tardy** *adj.*
earn deserve *vb.*
Earth world *n.*
easily *adv.*
easy *adj.*
easy **tough** *adj.*
easygoing **severe** *adj.*
ebb decrease *vb.*
edge **center** *n.*
edge *n.*
effect *n.*
effort labor *n.*
effortless easy *adj.*
effortlessly easily *adv.*
embrace adopt *vb.*
emerge appear *vb.*
emerge **dive** *vb.*
employ *vb.*

emptiness **matter** *n.*
empty vacant *adj.*
encircle enclose *vb.*
enclose insert *vb.*
enclose shelter *vb.*
enclose *vb.*
encompass enclose *vb.*
encourage **frighten** *vb.*
encourage **prevent** *vb.*
end **center** *n.*
end quit *vb.*
endure remain *vb.*
enemies **friends** *n.*
enemy **companion** *n.*
energetic **inactive** *adj.*
energy power *n.*
energy strength *n.*
engage employ *vb.*
enjoy love *vb.*
enjoyable *adj.*
enjoyable pleasant *adj.*
enjoyable **terrible** *adj.*
enjoyable wonderful *adj.*
enjoyment *n.*
enormous gigantic *adj.*
enormous huge *adj.*
enraged angry *adj.*
enraged furious *adj.*
ensemble outfit *n.*
enter insert *vb.*

KEY entry word = **bold red**   synonym = **bold black**
        antonym = light black   part of speech = *italic*

13

fade **disappear** *vb.*
fade **vanish** *vb.*
fail overcome *vb.*
fair carnival *n.*
fair unfair *adj.*
faith *n.*
faithless loyal *adj.*
false loyal *adj.*
falter hesitate *vb.*
familiar odd *adj.*
familiar strange *adj.*
familiar unknown *adj.*
fancy grand *adj.*
fancy plain *adj.*
far from near *prep.*
fascinate charm *vb.*
fascinating dull *adj.*
fascinating exciting *adj.*
fascinating wonderful
  adj.
fashion create *vb.*
fast quick *adj.*
fast quickly *adv.*
fasten join *vb.*
fasten *vb.*
fathomless deep *adj.*
fault mistake *n.*
faultless perfect *adj.*
faulty perfect *adj.*
favor *n.*
favorable wonderful
  adj.
fear *n.*

fearless afraid *adj.*
fearlessness fear *n.*
feast banquet *n.*
feat adventure *n.*
feature quality *n.*
federation union *n.*
feeble mighty *adj.*
feeble weak *adj.*
feebleness strength *n.*
feed nourish *vb.*
fickle loyal *adj.*
fierce mild *adj.*
fight argument *n.*
fight *vb.*
file sort *vb.*
filled vacant *adj.*
final *adj.*
find locate *vb.*
fine keen *adj.*
fine rough *adj.*
finish quit *vb.*
finish *vb.*
fire employ *vb.*
first final *adj.*
flabbergast amaze *vb.*
flare glare *n.*
flare *n.*
flash flare *n.*
flash glare *n.*
flash *n.*
flat exciting *adj.*
flaw *n.*

KEY entry word = **bold red**   synonym = **bold black**
      antonym = light black   part of speech = *italic*

flawed **perfect** *adj.*
flawless **perfect** *adj.*
fled *vb.*
flimsy **weak** *adj.*
fling **throw** *vb.*
flock **horde** *n.*
fluctuate **vary** *vb.*
foam *n.*
foe **companion** *n.*
follow **obey** *vb.*
follow **understand** *vb.*
foolish *adj.*
forbid **permit** *vb.*
forbid **require** *vb.*
force **order** *vb.*
force **power** *n.*
force **strength** *n.*
force *vb.*
forceful **mighty** *adj.*
forever **always** *adv.*
forget **recall** *vb.*
form **create** *vb.*
fragrance **perfume** *n.*
frail **mighty** *adj.*
frail **weak** *adj.*
frayed **worn** *adj.*
freedom **independence** *n.*
freezing **cold** *adj.*
frequent *adj.*
frequently **often** *adv.*
fresh **brand-new** *adj.*
fresh **modern** *adj.*

fresh **weary** *adj.*
friend **companion** *n.*
friends *n.*
fright **fear** *n.*
frighten **scare** *vb.*
frighten *vb.*
frightened **afraid** *adj.*
frigid **cold** *adj.*
frivolous **foolish** *adj.*
frontier **border** *n.*
frosty **cold** *adj.*
frosty **frozen** *adj.*
froth **foam** *n.*
frown *vb.*
frozen *adj.*
fry **boil** *vb.*
full **vacant** *adj.*
fully **barely** *adv.*
fuming **angry** *adj.*
fun **entertainment** *n.*
functional **practical** *adj.*
fundamental **basic** *adj.*
furious *adj.*
furious **angry** *adj.*
furnish **provide** *vb.*
fussy **plain** *adj.*

G

gain *vb.*
gale wind *n.*
garbage *n.*
garbage waste *n.*
gather marshal *vb.*
gather scatter *vb.*
gathering group *n.*
gathering horde *n.*
gave away kept *vb.*
gaze peer *vb.*
gem jewel *n.*
generate create *vb.*
gentle *adj.*
gesture signal *n.*
get receive *vb.*
giant huge *adj.*
gigantic *adj.*
gigantic huge *adj.*
giggle laugh *vb.*
gingerly carefully *adv.*
gist kernel *n.*
give receive *vb.*
give grab *vb.*
give *vb.*
glad jolly *adj.*
glad unhappy *adj.*
glare flare *n.*
glare frown *vb.*

glare *n.*
glassy slippery *adj.*
gleam brighten *vb.*
gleam flash *n.*
glide prowl *vb.*
glittering bright *adj.*
globe world *n.*
gloomy unhappy *adj.*
glorious grand *adj.*
glowing bright *adj.*
go away return *vb.*
go leave *vb.*
go quit *vb.*
go reach *vb.*
goal *n.*
goal purpose *n.*
goes *vb.*
good manners courtesy *n.*
good naughty *adj.*
grab *vb.*
grand *adj.*
grant deny *vb.*
grasp understand *vb.*
grasped knew *vb.*
grateful *adj.*
gratify bother *vb.*
gratifying wonderful *adj.*
greasy oily *adj.*
great huge *adj.*

heart **inside** *n.*
hearten **frighten** *vb.*
heartless **mean** *adj.*
heated **angry** *adj.*
heave **raise** *vb.*
heckle **bother** *vb.*
heed **listen** *vb.*
heed **notice** *vb.*
heedlessly **carefully** *adv.*
held **kept** *vb.*
help **hamper** *vb.*
help **harm** *vb.*
helpful **useful** *adj.*
hesitate *vb.*
hid *vb.*
hidden *adj.*
hidden **secret** *adj.*
hide **shelter** *vb.*
higher **major** *adj.*
hinder **hamper** *vb.*
hinder **prevent** *vb.*
hire **employ** *vb.*
hiss **noise** *n.*
hodgepodge **variety** *n.*
hoist *vb.*
holidays **vacation** *n.*
honor **celebrate** *vb.*
honor *vb.*
hop **jump** *vb.*
horde *n.*
horrible **terrible** *adj.*

horrify **frighten** *vb.*
hot **cold** *adj.*
hot **frozen** *adj.*
hover **loom** *vb.*
howl **laugh** *vb.*
howl *n.*
howl **scream** *vb.*
huge *adj.*
huge **gigantic** *adj.*
hullabaloo **racket** *n.*
human **person** *n.*
humid **damp** *adj.*
humility **pride** *n.*
hurry **loiter** *vb.*
hurry *n.*
hurry **rush** *vb.*
hurt **cure** *vb.*
hurt **harm** *vb.*
hurtful **harmful** *adj.*
hush **racket** *n.*
hushed **quiet** *adj.*

icy **cold** *adj.*
icy **frozen** *adj.*
icy **slippery** *adj.*
ideal **perfect** *adj.*
identical **twin** *adj.*
ignore **adopt** *vb.*
ignore **celebrate** *vb.*
ignore **listen** *vb.*

KEY entry word = **bold red** synonym = **bold black**
antonym = light black part of speech = *italic*

19

instrument *n.*
intelligent foolish *adj.*
intelligent smart *adj.*
intended meant *vb.*
intention purpose *n.*
interested curious *adj.*
interesting dull *adj.*
interesting exciting *adj.*
interfere with hamper *vb.*
interior border *n.*
interior inside *n.*
interior outside *n.*
invent create *vb.*
investigate explore *vb.*
invincible mighty *adj.*
irk bother *vb.*
irrational foolish *adj.*
irregular uneven *adj.*
irritate bother *vb.*
irritated angry *adj.*
issue question *n.*
issue subject *n.*

jagged rough *adj.*
jangle noise *n.*
jealous *adj.*
jewel *n.*
jingle noise *n.*
job chore *n.*

join scatter *vb.*
join *vb.*
jolly *adj.*
jot note *vb.*
journal *n.*
journey *n.*
journey travel *vb.*
journey voyage *n.*
joy *n.*
joyful furious *adj.*
joyful unhappy *adj.*
joyful wonderful *adj.*
jumbo huge *adj.*
jump *vb.*
just unfair *adj.*

keen *adj.*
keep own *vb.*
kept *vb.*
kernel *n.*
key basic *adj.*
key major *adj.*
kind mean *adj.*
kind nature *n.*
kind severe *adj.*
kind type *n.*
kindness favor *n.*
knew *vb.*
knife *n.*
knock *vb.*

lose gain *vb.*

lose locate *vb.*

lose overcome *vb.*

lost kept *vb.*

loud *adj.*

loud quiet *adj.*

loud silent *adj.*

loudly quietly *adv.*

love *vb.*

lower raise *vb.*

loyal *adj.*

loyalty *n.*

ludicrous foolish *adj.*

lug carry *vb.*

lure *vb.*

lurk prowl *vb.*

lying *vb.*

mad angry *adj.*

made built *vb.*

made-to-order ready-made *adj.*

magnificent grand *adj.*

major *adj.*

major important *adj.*

make ill cure *vb.*

make up fight *vb.*

mammoth gigantic *adj.*

mammoth huge *adj.*

manager boss *n.*

maneuver *vb.*

mannerly impolite *adj.*

manufacture *vb.*

manufactured ready-made *adj.*

march prowl *vb.*

march *vb.*

mark dot *n.*

mark notice *vb.*

mark *n.*

marred perfect *adj.*

marshal *vb.*

marvelous wonderful *adj.*

masked secret *adj.*

mass group *n.*

mass heap *n.*

mass horde *n.*

mass matter *n.*

mass-produced ready-made *adj.*

massive huge *adj.*

matching equal *adj.*

matching twin *adj.*

material matter *n.*

matter *n.*

mature grown-up *adj.*

mean *adj.*

meander roam *vb.*

meant *vb.*

mechanism instrument *n.*

medal prize *n.*

KEY	entry word = **bold red**	synonym = **bold black**
	antonym = light black	part of speech = *italic*

medal trophy *n.*

melody song *n.*

menace danger *n.*

menace threat *n.*

mend sew *vb.*

mends patches *vb.*

merit deserve *vb.*

merrily happily *adv.*

merry jolly *adj.*

merry unhappy *adj.*

microscopic gigantic *adj.*

middle *adj.*

middle center *n.*

middle edge *n.*

midpoint center *n.*

mighty *adj.*

mild *adj.*

mild cold *adj.*

mild severe *adj.*

mimic tease *vb.*

minor important *adj.*

minor major *adj.*

minute gigantic *adj.*

minute tall *adj.*

mischievous naughty *adj.*

miserable unhappy *adj.*

misinformed mistaken *adj.*

miss locate *vb.*

miss overlook *vb.*

missing absent *adj.*

mission *n.*

missions errands *n.*

mistake *n.*

mistaken *adj.*

moan laugh *vb.*

mob horde *n.*

mock honor *vb.*

modern *adj.*

modern prehistoric *adj.*

modesty pride *n.*

modify vary *vb.*

moist *adj.*

moist damp *adj.*

money wealth *n.*

monstrous huge *adj.*

monumental gigantic *adj.*

mope laugh *vb.*

motion signal *n.*

mountainous gigantic *adj.*

mournfully happily *adv.*

moves goes *vb.*

moving exciting *adj.*

mud dirt *n.*

muffled quiet *adj.*

multiply limit *vb.*

multitude horde *n.*

murmur howl *n.*

murmur roar *vb.*

murmur scream *vb.*

muscular mighty *adj.*

muscular weak *adj.*

must **ought** *vb.*
mustn't **ought** *vb.*
muted quiet *adj.*
myriads horde *n.*
mysterious secret *adj.*
mysterious unknown *adj.*

nag bother *vb.*
nap *vb.*
narrow *adj.*
narrow limit *vb.*
natural *adj.*
nature *n.*
naughty *adj.*
near *prep.*
nearby *adj.*
necessary **unnecessary** *adj.*
needed unnecessary *adj.*
needless unnecessary *adj.*
neglect celebrate *vb.*
neglect overlook *vb.*
neighborhood *n.*
neighboring nearby *adj.*
never **always** *adv.*
never **often** *adv.*
new modern *adj.*
new **prehistoric** *adj.*

nice **mean** *adj.*
noise *n.*
noiseless **loud** *adj.*
noiseless quiet *adj.*
noiseless silent *adj.*
noisily **quietly** *adv.*
noisy loud *adj.*
noisy **quiet** *adj.*
noisy **silent** *adj.*
none nothing *n.*
nonsensical foolish *adj.*
nonskid slippery *adj.*
normal natural *adj.*
note *vb.*
noteworthy special *adj.*
nothing matter *n.*
nothing *n.*
notice overlook *vb.*
notice *vb.*
notion *n.*
nourish *vb.*
novel modern *adj.*
novel *n.*
numerous frequent *adj.*

obedient **naughty** *adj.*
obey order *vb.*
obey *vb.*
objection protest *n.*
objective goal *n.*

parched moist adj.

particularly especially adv.

partly quite adv.

pass give vb.

patches vb.

path course n.

path n.

pause hesitate vb.

pause quit vb.

pay attention to overlook vb.

peaceful calm adj.

peaceful furious adj.

pebble rock n.

pedestrian adj.

peer vb.

peeved angry adj.

perfect adj.

perfume n.

permit prevent vb.

permit vb.

person n.

perturb bother vb.

pester bother vb.

petrify frighten vb.

pickup van n.

pier n.

pile group n.

pile heap n.

pinpoint locate vb.

pitch throw vb.

pitch-dark dark adj.

place lay vb.

plain adj.

plain grand adj.

plan create vb.

planet world n.

planned meant vb.

plate n.

platter plate n.

pleasant adj.

pleasant awful adj.

pleasant enjoyable adj.

pleasant terrible adj.

pleasant wonderful adj.

please annoy vb.

please bother vb.

please disappoint vb.

please worry vb.

pleased angry adj.

pleasing wonderful adj.

pleasurable wonderful adj.

pleasure enjoyment n.

pledge promise n.

plot maneuver vb.

plunge dive vb.

poetry verse n.

point dot n.

poison cure vb.

polite impolite adj.

politeness courtesy n.

KEY entry word = **bold red** synonym = **bold black**
antonym = light black part of speech = *italic*

pop noise n.
portion section n.
portray describe vb.
positive certain adj.
possess own vb.
potent mighty adj.
pouch bag n.
pound knock vb.
poverty wealth n.
power n.
power strength n.
powerful mighty adj.
powerful strong adj.
powerful weak adj.
powerless strong adj.
practical adj.
praise honor vb.
precious stone jewel n.
precise exact adj.
predicted sudden adj.
prehistoric adj.
prepared ready adj.
present absent adj.
present give vb.
present modern adj.
pressing urgent adj.
prevent vb.
pride n.
primarily especially adv.
primary major adj.
primitive prehistoric adj.
print write vb.

prize n.
prize trophy n.
problem question n.
problem subject n.
problem trouble n.
proceeds goes vb.
produce create vb.
produce manufacture vb.
profusion quantity n.
prohibit allow vb.
prohibit permit vb.
prohibit require vb.
prolonged sudden adj.
promise n.
prompt tardy adj.
promptly immediately adv.
property wealth n.
propose offer vb.
protect harm vb.
protect shelter vb.
protest n.
provide vb.
provoke bother vb.
prowl vb.
prune shear vb.
prying curious adj.
pull haul vb.
punch knock vb.
punctures patches vb.
purpose goal n.
purpose n.

quality *n.*
quantity *n.*
quarrel argument *n.*
quarrel fight *vb.*
quarrel *n.*
question *n.*
quick *adj.*
quick sudden *adj.*
quickly *adv.*
quickly rapidly *adv.*
quiet *adj.*
quiet loud *adj.*
quiet noise *n.*
quiet racket *n.*
quiet silent *adj.*
quietly *adv.*
quit *vb.*
quite *adv.*
quiver tremble *vb.*

racket noise *n.*
racket *n.*
ragged worn *adj.*
raging angry *adj.*
raise hoist *vb.*
raise *vb.*
ramble roam *vb.*

ranking major *adj.*
rap knock *vb.*
rapid quick *adj.*
rapidly *adv.*
rapidly quickly *adv.*
rare frequent *adj.*
rare special *adj.*
rarely always *adv.*
rarely often *adv.*
reach *vb.*
readily immediately
  adv.
ready *adj.*
ready-made *adj.*
realistic practical *adj.*
realize learn *vb.*
really *adv.*
reappear disappear
  vb.
reappear vanish *vb.*
reason purpose *n.*
reasonable practical
  adj.
reassure alarm *vb.*
reassure frighten *vb.*
reassure scare *vb.*
reassure worry *vb.*
rebuff deny *vb.*
recall *vb.*
receive *vb.*
recent modern *adj.*
recess vacation *n.*

revealed **hid** vb.
revealed **secret** adj.
reverberation racket n.
revisit return vb.
rhyme verse n.
riches wealth n.
ridicule tease vb.
ridiculous foolish adj.
right unfair adj.
right **wrong** adj.
rim edge n.
ring enclose vb.
ripe ready adj.
rips **patches** vb.
risk danger n.
river n.
road path n.
roam vb.
roam travel vb.
roar laugh vb.
roar noise n.
roar racket n.
roar scream vb.
roar vb.
rock n.
rope yarn n.
rotate whirl vb.
rough adj.
rough gentle adj.
rough mild adj.
rough slippery adj.
rough uneven adj.
rousing exciting adj.

route course n.
route path n.
rove roam vb.
row n.
rubbish garbage n.
rubbish waste n.
ruby scarlet adj.
rude grateful adj.
rude impolite adj.
rudeness
    courtesy n.
rush hurry n.
rush loiter vb.
rush vb.

sack bag n.
sad jolly adj.
sad unhappy adj.
sadly happily adv.
sadness joy n.
safe harmful adj.
safe vault n.
safe-deposit box vault
    n.
safeguard shelter vb.
safety danger n.
said told vb.
sanction adopt vb.
satisfy disappoint vb.
satisfying wonderful
    adj.

31

saucer plate *n.*
saved kept *vb.*
scalpel knife *n.*
scarcely barely *adv.*
scare alarm *vb.*
scare fear *n.*
scare *vb.*
scared afraid *adj.*
scarlet *adj.*
scatter *vb.*
scent perfume *n.*
scheme maneuver *vb.*
scorn respect *vb.*
scowl frown *vb.*
scrap waste *n.*
scratch mark *n.*
scream howl *n.*
scream roar *vb.*
scream *vb.*
screech howl *n.*
screech scream *vb.*
screen shelter *vb.*
scribble note *vb.*
scribble write *vb.*
seasoned grown-up *adj.*
secret *adj.*
secret hidden *adj.*
secreted hid *vb.*
section *n.*
secure slippery *adj.*
segment section *n.*
seize grab *vb.*
seldom always *adv.*

sensational exciting *adj.*
senseless foolish *adj.*
sensible practical *adj.*
separate fasten *vb.*
separate join *vb.*
serious jolly *adj.*
serviceable practical *adj.*
set lay *vb.*
set out leave *vb.*
settled uncertain *adj.*
settlement argument *n.*
settlement quarrel *n.*
severe *adj.*
sew *vb.*
shabby worn *adj.*
shade shadows *n.*
shaded dark *adj.*
shadows *n.*
shake tremble *vb.*
shaky weak *adj.*
shallow deep *adj.*
shape affect *vb.*
shape create *vb.*
sharp keen *adj.*
shear *vb.*
shell outside *n.*
shelter *vb.*
shield shelter *vb.*
shift vary *vb.*
shiny bright *adj.*
shiver tremble *vb.*

short **tall** *adj.*
shortcoming flaw *n.*
should ought *vb.*
shouldn't **ought** *vb.*
shout howl *n.*
shout laugh *vb.*
shout roar *vb.*
shout scream *vb.*
show appear *vb.*
showed **hid** *vb.*
showed taught *vb.*
shriek howl *n.*
shriek laugh *vb.*
shriek scream *vb.*
shrink decline *vb.*
shrink decrease *vb.*
shut down quit *vb.*
shut **open** *adj.*
sickly weak *adj.*
side edge *n.*
sign signal *n.*
signal *n.*
significant important *adj.*
silence **noise** *n.*
silence **racket** *n.*
silent *adj.*
silent **loud** *adj.*
silent quiet *adj.*
silently quietly *adv.*
silky **rough** *adj.*
silly foolish *adj.*
similar equal *adj.*

simmer **boil** *vb.*
simple easy *adj.*
simple plain *adj.*
simple **tough** *adj.*
single **twin** *adj.*
singly alone *adv.*
sitting **lying** *vb.*
sizable huge *adj.*
sizable tall *adj.*
skills abilities *n.*
skin **inside** *n.*
skin **outside** *n.*
skip jump *vb.*
skip overlook *vb.*
skulk prowl *vb.*
sleepy weary *adj.*
slender narrow *adj.*
slice section *n.*
slick slippery *adj.*
slightly **quite** *adv.*
slim narrow *adj.*
slimy oily *adj.*
slink prowl *vb.*
slippery *adj.*
sloppy **careful** *adj.*
slow down **rush** *vb.*
slow **quick** *adj.*
slowly **immediately** *adv.*
slowly **quickly** *adv.*
slowly **rapidly** *adv.*
sluggish inactive *adj.*
sluggish **quick** *adj.*

KEY entry word = **bold red**   synonym = **bold black**
antonym = light black   part of speech = *italic*

stack heap *n.*	**story** tale *n.*
stain mark *n.*	straight bent *adj.*
stale brand-new *adj.*	**strange** *adj.*
standing lying *vb.*	**strange** odd *adj.*
stare peer *vb.*	**strange** unknown *adj.*
start finish *vb.*	stranger companion *n.*
start quit *vb.*	strangers friends *n.*
startle alarm *vb.*	**streak** mark *n.*
startle scare *vb.*	**stream** river *n.*
startling sudden *adj.*	**street** path *n.*
stay leave *vb.*	**strength** *n.*
stay remain *vb.*	**strew** scatter *vb.*
stay travel *vb.*	**strict** severe *adj.*
stayed fled *vb.*	**stride** prowl *vb.*
stays goes *vb.*	**string** yarn *n.*
steadfastness loyalty *n.*	**stroke** mark *n.*
steal prowl *vb.*	stroll rush *vb.*
stealthily quietly *adv.*	**strong** *adj.*
steaming frozen *adj.*	**strong** mighty *adj.*
steamy cold *adj.*	strong mild *adj.*
step march *vb.*	strong weak *adj.*
stern severe *adj.*	**struggle** battle *n.*
still quiet *adj.*	**strut** prowl *vb.*
stir racket *n.*	**study** explore *vb.*
stirring exciting *adj.*	**stun** amaze *vb.*
stitch sew *vb.*	sturdy weak *adj.*
stone rock *n.*	**subject** *n.*
stop finish *vb.*	**subside** decline *vb.*
stop prevent *vb.*	**subside** decrease *vb.*
stop quit *vb.*	**substance** kernel *n.*
stop travel *vb.*	**substance** matter *n.*
stops goes *vb.*	**sudden** *adj.*
story novel *n.*	**suds** foam *n.*

KEY	entry word = **bold red**	synonym = **bold black**
	antonym = light black	part of speech = *italic*

suggest offer *vb.*
suggest order *vb.*
sunlit dark *adj.*
superfluous basic *adj.*
**superfluous
  unnecessary** *adj.*
superhuman mighty
  adj.
superior major *adj.*
superior special *adj.*
supply provide *vb.*
suppose guess *vb.*
suppose imagine *vb.*
suppose wonder *vb.*
sure certain *adj.*
sure uncertain *adj.*
surface dive *vb.*
surpass overcome *vb.*
surrender give *vb.*
surrender overcome
  vb.
surround enclose *vb.*
surround shelter *vb.*
suspicions faith *n.*
sustain nourish *vb.*
swagger prowl *vb.*
swarm horde *n.*
sway affect *vb.*
swiftly rapidly *adv.*
swoop dive *vb.*

take apart join *vb.*

take carry *vb.*
take down raise *vb.*
take give *vb.*
take out insert *vb.*
tale *n.*
tale novel *n.*
talents abilities *n.*
talk discussion *n.*
tall *adj.*
tap knock *vb.*
tardily immediately
  adv.
tardy *adj.*
task chore *n.*
tasks errands *n.*
taught *vb.*
taunt tease *vb.*
team group *n.*
tears patches *vb.*
tease *vb.*
tedious dull *adj.*
tempt lure *vb.*
tender gentle *adj.*
terrible *adj.*
terrible awful *adj.*
terrific wonderful *adj.*
terrified afraid *adj.*
terrify frighten *vb.*
terrify scare *vb.*
terror fear *n.*
thankful grateful *adj.*
theory notion *n.*
thin narrow *adj.*

thorough careful *adj.*
thoughtful careless *adj.*
thoughtless careless *adj.*
thrashing upset *n.*
thread yarn *n.*
threadbare worn *adj.*
threat *n.*
threaten loom *vb.*
thrill amaze *vb.*
thrilling exciting *adj.*
throng horde *n.*
throw *vb.*
thwart prevent *vb.*
time date *n.*
tiny gigantic *adj.*
tiny huge *adj.*
tiny tall *adj.*
tired weary *adj.*
tiresome dull *adj.*
together alone *adv.*
toil labor *n.*
told *vb.*
took flight fled *vb.*
tool instrument *n.*
top lid *n.*
topic question *n.*
topic subject *n.*
tore down built *vb.*
tornado wind *n.*
toss throw *vb.*
tough *adj.*

tough mighty *adj.*
tough strong *adj.*
tour voyage *n.*
tow drag *vb.*
towering gigantic *adj.*
towering huge *adj.*
towering tall *adj.*
town village *n.*
trail path *n.*
trait quality *n.*
tramp march *vb.*
tranquil calm *adj.*
transform vary *vb.*
trash garbage *n.*
trash waste *n.*
travel *vb.*
treasure jewel *n.*
treat cure *vb.*
trek journey *n.*
tremble *vb.*
tremendous gigantic *adj.*
tremendous huge *adj.*
trim shear *vb.*
trip journey *n.*
trip voyage *n.*
trivial important *adj.*
trophy *n.*
trophy prize *n.*
trouble *n.*
troublesome tough *adj.*
truck van *n.*
true loyal *adj.*

KEY entry word = bold red   synonym = **bold black**
antonym = light black   part of speech = *italic*

37

true **wrong** *adj.*
trust depend *vb.*
trust faith *n.*
trusty loyal *adj.*
tug haul *vb.*
tumbledown weak *adj.*
tumult racket *n.*
tune song *n.*
twin *adj.*
twine yarn *n.*
twinkle flash *n.*
twirl *vb.*
twisted bent *adj.*
type *n.*
typical natural *adj.*

unafraid **afraid** *adj.*
unauthorized **official** *adj.*
unbearable terrible *adj.*
uncertain *adj.*
uncertain **certain** *adj.*
unclosed open *adj.*
uncommon special *adj.*
uncommon **usual** *adj.*
uncover **shelter** *vb.*
uncovered **hid** *vb.*
uncovered open *adj.*
undecided uncertain *adj.*
undercover secret *adj.*

understand *vb.*
understanding **argument** *n.*
understanding knowledge *n.*
understanding **quarrel** *n.*
understood knew *vb.*
understood known *vb.*
undertaking venture *n.*
unenjoyable **pleasant** *adj.*
unequal **equal** *adj.*
unequal unfair *adj.*
uneven *adj.*
unexpected **natural** *adj.*
unexpected sudden *adj.*
unexpected **usual** *adj.*
unfair *adj.*
unfamiliar strange *adj.*
unfamiliar unknown *adj.*
unfasten **fasten** *vb.*
ungrateful **grateful** *adj.*
unhappily **happily** *adv.*
unhappiness **enjoyment** *n.*
unhappy *adj.*
unhappy **jolly** *adj.*
unhurriedly **quickly** *adv.*
unimportant **basic** *adj.*

unimportant
  important *adj.*

unimportant major
  adj.

uninterested curious
  adj.

union *n.*

unique special *adj.*

unite scatter *vb.*

unjust unfair *adj.*

unkind mean *adj.*

unknown *adj.*

unknown secret *adj.*

unknown strange *adj.*

unnatural natural *adj.*

unnecessary *adj.*

unnecessary basic *adj.*

unoccupied vacant *adj.*

unpleasant enjoyable
  adj.

unpleasant pleasant
  adj.

unpleasant wonderful
  adj.

unpredicted sudden
  adj.

unprepared ready *adj.*

unrealistic practical
  adj.

unremarkable special
  adj.

unripe ready *adj.*

unruffled calm *adj.*

unseasoned grown-up
  adj.

unsettled uncertain
  adj.

unspeaking quiet *adj.*

unsteady weak *adj.*

unsure certain *adj.*

unthinking careless *adj.*

untrue loyal *adj.*

untrue wrong *adj.*

unused brand-new *adj.*

unusual odd *adj.*

unusual usual *adj.*

unwise foolish *adj.*

unworkable practical
  adj.

unyielding mighty *adj.*

uphill tough *adj.*

uproar racket *n.*

upset *n.*

up-to-date modern *adj.*

up-to-the-minute
  modern *adj.*

urgent *adj.*

usable practical *adj.*

used brand-new *adj.*

useful *adj.*

useful unnecessary
  adj.

useless unnecessary
  adj.

useless worthy *adj.*

usual *adj.*

usual odd *adj.*

usual special *adj.*

usually often *adverb*

KEY   entry word = bold red   synonym = **bold black**
          antonym = light black   part of speech = *italic*

39

whirl **twirl** *vb.*
whirl *vb.*
whisper **howl** *n.*
whisper **roar** *vb.*
whisper **scream** *vb.*
whispery quiet *adj.*
whole **section** *n.*
wholly barely *adv.*
wholly quite *adv.*
whoop **scream** *vb.*
whopping huge *adj.*
wild **mild** *adj.*
wind *n.*
wind up **quit** *vb.*
wintry cold *adj.*
wise **foolish** *adj.*
wise **smart** *adj.*
withheld secret *adj.*
woefully happily *adv.*
wonder *vb.*
wonderful *adj.*
wonderful **awful** *adj.*
wonderful **terrible** *adj.*
word **promise** *n.*
work **labor** *n.*
workable **practical** *adj.*
world *n.*
worn *adj.*
worn-out **weary** *adj.*
worry **bother** *vb.*
worry **trouble** *n.*
worry *vb.*

worthless **worthy** *adj.*
worthwhile worthy *adj.*
worthy *adj.*
wrecked **built** *vb.*
write *vb.*
wrong *adj.*
wrong **exact** *adj.*
wrong unfair *adj.*

yarn *n.*
yell **howl** *n.*
yell **roar** *vb.*
yell **scream** *vb.*
youthful **grown-up** *adj.*
yowl howl *n.*

zero **nothing** *n.*

abilities *n.,* pl. of ability. powers to do or
to act:
>My teacher believes that all people have
>artistic *abilities*.

skills powers or abilities to do something:
>Marta's writing *skills* helped her win the
>poetry contest.

aptitudes natural abilities or talents:
>Barry shows *aptitudes* for music and math.

talents special natural abilities or aptitudes:
>The *talents* of many actors contributed to
>the movie's success.

absent *adj.* not in a place at a certain time:
>Two senators were *absent* from the
>meeting.

away in another place; absent:
>Mercedes called Ron, but he was *away* at
>the time.

missing absent or lacking:
>One of the pieces for the toy is *missing*
>from the box.

adopt *v.* to accept or approve, especially by
formal vote:
>The mayor hopes the citizens will *adopt*
>the plan.

approve to have a favorable opinion toward
or give consent to:
>Most of the club members *approve* the list
>of rules.

sanction to give approval or support to:

Many businesses *sanction* the use of
recycled paper.

embrace to take up as one's own, to adopt:
Today, many countries *embrace* the idea of
conserving the environment.

adventure *n.* something that a person does
that is difficult or exciting:
The camping trip was an *adventure* for the
whole family.

exploit a brave deed or act:
The newspaper article described the
exploit of the rescue squad in great detail.

feat an act or deed that shows great
courage, strength, or skill:
Crossing the river on horseback was a *feat*
for even the strongest rider.

venture a task or undertaking that involves
risk or danger:
Taking part in a *venture* such as the search
for a sunken ship needs great courage.

advice *n.* an opinion that helps someone make
a decision or take action:
Helen asked her aunt's *advice* about
the problem.

counsel thoughtful opinion:
The man's wise *counsel* gave the
villagers hope.

guidance something that guides or gives
direction:
Jeremy asked Mrs. Quinn for *guidance* in
choosing next year's classes.

affect *v.* to act upon:
>   Vitamins *affect* people's health in a
>   good way.

influence to produce an effect:
>   A good teacher can *influence* the way a
>   student feels about learning.

shape to give a definite direction or
character to:
>   The books I read and admire often *shape*
>   the way I write.

sway to cause to be directed in a
certain way:
>   Guillermo did not let the TV ads *sway* his
>   opinions of the candidates.

afraid *adj.* fearful:
>   Are you *afraid* of the dark?

frightened afraid:
>   Ty was *frightened* by the loud thunder.

scared afraid:
>   I am *scared* of big dogs.

terrified filled with great fear:
>   My brother is *terrified* of snakes.

agree *v.* to say one is willing:
>   I *agree* to clean my room every Saturday.

consent to say yes:
>   I *consent* to your plan.

approve to agree to officially:
>   The committee will *approve* the use of
>   music in the cafeteria.

alarm *v.* to disturb or make afraid:
>   It didn't *alarm* me.

scare to make afraid:
>   This will *scare* my brother.

startle to take by surprise:
Storms *startle* our parrot.

alert *adj.* watching and listening carefully:
The deer was *alert* to every slight sound
in the forest.
attentive watching, listening, or
concentrating carefully:
The *attentive* student heard the directions
the first time.
observant noticing:
The *observant* witness remembered the
make and color of the speeding car.
watchful paying close attention:
The boy sat next to his sleeping baby
sister in *watchful* silence.
vigilant paying close attention, usually with
the idea of watching for danger:
The *vigilant* guards never fell asleep at
their posts.

allow *v.* to permit:
She will *allow* him to watch TV after his
homework is done.
let to give permission:
I will *let* you go later.
approve to officially agree to something:
Will your teacher *approve* the idea?

alone *adv.* by oneself:
The girl walked *alone* on the beach.
apart away from other people or things:
He sat *apart* from the rest of the team.
singly alone or one at a time:
The coach spoke to each of the team
members *singly*.

always *adv.* as long as possible:
> I will remember their kindness *always*.

forever for all time:
> Ned will be my friend *forever*.

continually without stop:
> My tooth aches *continually*.

---

amaze *v.* to surprise greatly; to fill with wonder.

astonish	flabbergast
astound	overwhelm
confound	stun
dazzle	thrill
excite	

- antonym: bore

---

angry *adj.* feeling or showing anger.

boiling	heated
cranky	irritated
enraged	mad
fuming	peeved
furious	raging

- antonyms: calm, happy, pleased

---

annoy *v.* to irritate:
> Too much noise will *annoy* me.

bother to pester:
> Don't *bother* me when I'm reading.

disturb to distract:
> Talking in the library will *disturb* others.

appear *v.* to come into sight:
> As soon as the first buds *appear,* she thinks it's spring.

emerge to come into view:
> In the night sky, the moon was trying to *emerge* from behind the scattered clouds.

show to be in sight, to be visible:
> If you use such thin cloth for the curtains, the light will *show* through them.

argument *n.* a discussion of something by people who do not agree:
> They had an *argument* about who was better at solving problems.

disagreement a difference of opinion:
> We resolved our *disagreement* by taking turns.

conflict a strong disagreement:
> Sometimes a minor problem can lead to a more serious *conflict.*

fight an angry disagreement:
> Let's not *fight* over which movie to see.

quarrel an angry argument or disagreement:
> The broken window set off a *quarrel* over who should get it fixed.

awful *adj.* very bad:
> It was an *awful* day for a picnic.

dreadful very frightening:
> The *dreadful* storm caused a lot of damage.

terrible unpleasant, possibly painful:
> Shawna has a *terrible* headache.

bag *n.* a container, often made from paper:
The *bag* is filled with apples.
sack a bag made of paper or fabric:
We gave a *sack* of old clothes to charity.
pouch a soft bag, often closed with string
or a flap:
A mail carrier carries a mail *pouch*.

banquet *n.* a large, elaborate, or formal meal:
My family had a *banquet* to celebrate my
great-grandmother's ninetieth birthday.
feast a fancy, plentiful meal, especially one
prepared for a special occasion:
There were sixty guests at the Kwans'
wedding *feast*.
dinner a formal meal in honor of a special
occasion:
The mayor attended the *dinner* held to
celebrate the new bridge.

barely *adv.* not much at all:
Kevin *barely* heard the whispered words.
hardly only just; barely:
The audience *hardly* noticed the player's
nervousness.
scarcely hardly:
Open the new carton of milk because this
carton has *scarcely* enough milk in it for
one bowl of cereal.

basic *adj.* forming the most important part:
Air, water, and food are *basic* needs
for life.

central very important, main:
  The *central* idea of the paragraph is
  usually found in the first sentence.
essential necessary:
  Extra water is *essential* if you want to hike
  in the desert during the summer.
fundamental serving as a basis, essential:
  Listening closely is a *fundamental* part of
  following directions.
key chief:
  The *key* ingredient of an enjoyable game is
  enthusiasm.

battle *n.* a fierce contest between people or
groups:
  The football game was a real *battle*.
struggle a contest of power or skill:
  The *struggle* between the teams ended
  in a tie.
conflict a strong disagreement:
  The two sides are in a bitter *conflict* over
  the issue.

believe *v.* to think something is true:
  Do you *believe* he is telling the truth?
accept to take as truth:
  He hoped she would *accept* his version of
  the events.
be convinced to be persuaded:
  Lu needs to *be convinced* that the plan
  is good.

bent *adj.* changed in shape:
  The *bent* nail won't hold the picture.
twisted bent or turned out of shape:
  A *twisted* straw is hard to drink with.

curved having no straight parts:

    You need a *curved* needle to fix the rip
    in the chair.

boil *v.* to make something so hot that steam
rises and bubbles from it:

    Boil the water before you put in the peas.

simmer to keep something heated just at or
below the boiling point:

    You should *simmer* the soup for an hour
    so the beans cook.

cook to use heat to make food ready to eat:

    After you *cook* the carrots, let them cool.

border *n.* a line where one area begins and
another ends:

    The train crossed the *border* between the
    United States and Canada.

boundary a line that marks the edge of a
country or state:

    The Rio Grande forms the *boundary*
    between the United States and Mexico.

frontier the far edge of a country, where it
borders on another country:

    As the train neared the *frontier,* guards
    came through to check our passports.

boss *n.* someone who plans and watches over
the work of others:

    My *boss* told me to work at the cash
    register today.

head a person who is above others in rank:

    The President is the *head* of our country's
    government.

chief someone with the highest rank of all:

The *chief* of the company should decide
how to run the business.

manager someone who watches over the
work of others in one part of a business:
   The company has three bookstores, and I
   am the *manager* of this one.

---

bother *v.* to give trouble to.

annoy	nag
disturb	perturb
exasperate	pester
heckle	provoke
irk	vex
irritate	worry

■ antonyms: please, charm, delight, gratify

---

bound *v.* to move quickly by jumping:
   A kangaroo can *bound* out of danger.
leap to make a big jump:
   You can *leap* across the narrow stream.
spring to move forward or jump up quickly:
   When Wu says "Surprise," we will *spring*
   from our hiding places.
vault to jump over:
   Laura's speed and strength helped her
   vault the railing.

brand-new *adj.* entirely new; newly made or
obtained:
   Some of my clothes are hand-me-downs
   from my big sisters, but I just got *brand-
   new* jeans.
unused never used before:

I knew by looking at the soles that these
sneakers were your *unused* pair and not
your old ones.

fresh newly done, made, gathered, or
obtained:

Instead of writing on that yellowed old
paper, open a *fresh* package.

bright *adj.* giving off light:

The sun is very *bright* today.

glowing shining:

The *glowing* candle filled the room with
soft light.

brilliant very bright, sparkling:

At dawn we saw the sun's *brilliant* light
across the water.

shiny reflecting light:

We waxed the car to make it *shiny*.

glittering sparkling:

The dress was covered with *glittering*
silver sequins.

brighten *v.* to gain more light:

We hoped the tunnel would *brighten* as
we got closer to the end.

blaze to shine or burn brightly:

I threw dry wood on the fire to make it
blaze so that I could see their faces better.

lighten

The weary walkers were glad to see the
sky *lighten* as the sun rose.

gleam to shine or glow:

The dirty lamp began to *gleam* as Aladdin
rubbed it with an old rag.

built *v.* past tense and past participle of build; put together parts and material:

They *built* the tree house yesterday.

made built or prepared:

Andrea *made* a salad.

constructed put up:

The school was *constructed* in 1912.

burden *n.* something that is carried:

The pile of books seemed like a heavy *burden* for such a small child to carry.

load a burden:

It was a great relief to transfer the heavy *load* from my back into the truck.

weight something heavy:

The sleeping cat was an unmoving *weight* on my lap.

calm *adj.* free from excitement or other strong feeling:

The teacher's *calm* manner put the students at ease.

tranquil free from disturbance:

Because there was no wind, the surface of the pond was smooth and *tranquil.*

peaceful calm:

The children were very excitable in the morning and argued constantly, but after lunch they were in a far more *peaceful* mood and played together quietly.

unruffled not disturbed:

Ray's *unruffled* reply showed that he was not angry at all.

careful *adj.* done with close attention:
> She made a *careful* check of the electric wires.

thorough leaving nothing out; careful and complete:
> Please do a *thorough* job of cleaning the desk.

detailed dealing with all the little parts of something:
> Roger made a *detailed* drawing of the rabbit.

cautious using close care:
> Sally was *cautious* when she walked across the narrow bridge.

carefully *adv.* paying close attention to avoid danger or risk:
> The tourists stayed *carefully* away from the edge of the cliff.

cautiously using care:
> The bicyclist *cautiously* avoided the potholes.

gingerly with great delicacy or care:
> *Gingerly,* I pulled the cactus spine from my thumb.

warily with care and caution:
> The mouse *warily* poked its nose out of the cupboard in case the cat was near.

careless *adj.* not paying enough attention; not cautious:
> The baseball player's *careless* swing resulted in a foul ball.

thoughtless careless:
> A *thoughtless* mistake in a math problem will give you an incorrect answer.

inattentive not paying attention:

The *inattentive* boy almost walked into the closed door.

unthinking not thinking or not careful:

Unthinking visitors left litter in the park.

carnival *n.* a festival that has games, rides, and shows:

She won a teddy bear at the *carnival*.

circus a show with trained animals, acrobats, and clowns:

We saw animals at the *circus*.

fair an outdoor show with entertainment:

Jody rode the rollercoaster at the *fair*.

carry *v.* to hold something to move it from place to place:

I will *carry* the pillows upstairs.

take to hold something and go with it to another place:

Take a sweater with you to the park.

haul to move something large or heavy from place to place:

The truck will *haul* the logs to the factory.

lug to move something with great effort:

I had to *lug* that heavy suitcase all the way to the bus stop.

cave *n.* a natural hollow space in the ground or in the side of a mountain:

Bears sleep in a *cave* for most of the winter.

cavern a large cave, often underground:

We explored a *cavern* deep in the ground.

burrow a hole in the ground made by an animal for shelter:

The rabbits lived in a *burrow*.

celebrate *v.* to show respect to a person or event with ceremonies or other activities:

We *celebrate* the birthday of George Washington because he was an important man in our country's history.

honor to remember a person or event with respect:

These ceremonies *honor* the people from our town who fought in World War I.

commemorate to honor or maintain the memory of:

The mayor declared a holiday to *commemorate* the founding of the town.

center *n.* a point the same distance from all points on the edge:

The circus ringmaster stood in the *center* of the ring.

midpoint in the middle, halfway:

The sailors reached the *midpoint* in their journey.

middle in between:

When you look at the children in the back row of the photo, Todd is the one in the *middle*.

core the center part:

The *core* of an apple contains the seeds.

certain *adj.* feeling no doubt:

Are you *certain* that Mabel is coming?

sure certain:

I am *sure* he can do the job.

positive certain:

I am *positive* that she is the fastest runner.

charm *v.* to attract or please greatly:

My little brother can *charm* most adults just by smiling at them.

fascinate to attract and hold the close interest of:

Mobiles with bright shapes usually *fascinate* young babies.

captivate to capture and hold the attention or affection of:

I have seen my grandfather *captivate* an audience with stories of his life.

chore *n.* something that has to be done regularly:

Setting the table is a *chore* I have to do every evening before I watch television.

job a specific piece of work:

The chart shows which student has the *job* of cleaning the hamster cage every day.

task a piece of work to be done:

Cleaning the chalkboard is a *task* I enjoy.

duty an action or service assigned to someone:

It's my *duty* to check that the plants are watered every third day.

club *n.* a group of people who meet for fun or a special purpose:

Jake and his friends decided to start a puzzle *club* to read and solve mysteries.

circle a group of people who have interests that they share and enjoy together:

Gerri is a member of a quilting *circle* that meets on the third Saturday of every month.

association a group of people joined together for a common purpose:

For many years Eli's family has belonged to an *association* of community volunteers.

---

cold *adj.* without warmth or heat.

chilly	**freezing**
cool	**frosty**
crisp	**icy**
frigid	**wintry**

■antonyms: hot, warm, steamy, mild

---

companion *n.* a person who keeps company with another; a friend:

In stories, the hero or heroine often has a *companion* with whom to share adventures.

friend a person who is known well and regarded with fondness:

Carlota has been my *friend* since preschool.

pal an informal word for a friend:

Fred's *pal* Nathan lives next door to him.

course *n.* the way to get somewhere:

The storm pushed the ship off its *course*.

route the way to get from one place to another:

We drove along the ocean *route* to the beach.

path a narrow road that leads from one place to another:

She followed the *path* back to camp.

courtesy *n.* courteous behavior; politeness:

Parents can encourage their children to treat other people with *courtesy*.

politeness having good or correct social behavior:

> The shopkeeper's *politeness* made her store very popular with customers.

good manners a good way of acting or behaving:

> People with *good manners* tend to get along well with each other.

---

create *v.* to bring into being.

build	generate
compose	invent
design	originate
dream up	plan
fashion	produce
form	shape

■ antonyms: destroy, copy

---

cure *v.* to bring back health:

> Rest will help *cure* that strained back.

heal to make better:

> A doctor's job is to *heal* the sick.

treat to take care of an illness or injury:

> A doctor should *treat* a high fever.

curious *adj.* eager to learn about something:

> I am *curious* about new inventions.

interested wanting to find out about something:

> Miguel is *interested* in the habits of whales.

prying looking or inquiring too closely:

> I have been told that *prying* into someone's personal life can be impolite.

damp *adj.* a little wet:
> The benches were still *damp* from the morning rain.

moist slightly wet:
> I cleaned the blackboard with a *moist* cloth.

humid having a lot of water vapor in the air:
> The air outside the museum was hot and *humid.*

dank uncomfortably wet and chilly:
> The cellar was dark and *dank* and smelled bad.

danger *n.* a chance of harm or injury:
> Fire is a *danger* to forests.

risk a chance of loss or harm:
> Firefighters often place their lives at *risk.*

hazard something that can cause injury:
> Bad weather can be a traffic *hazard.*

menace a person or thing that is a threat:
> Careless drivers are a *menace.*

dark *adj.* having little or no light:
> It was a very *dark* night.

pitch-dark so dark one cannot see:
> It was *pitch-dark* in the forest that night.

dim having very little light:
> We could hardly see the chairs and tables in the *dim* room.

shaded where light is blocked out:
> We walked in the *shaded* area under the trees.

date *n.* the day on which something happens:
What is the *date* of your birthday?
time a specific hour or minute:
At what *time* are we having lunch?
appointment an arranged time for a meeting:
I have an *appointment* at 4 o'clock.

---

decrease *v.* to become less.

decline	**shrink**
diminish	**subside**
dwindle	**wane**
ebb	**waste away**
fade	
lessen	

▪ antonyms: increase, grow, expand

---

deep *adj.* far down from the surface or top:
The Pacific Ocean is very *deep*.
bottomless so deep it doesn't seem to have a bottom:
He threw a pebble down into the *bottomless* well and never heard it splash.
fathomless so deep it seems impossible to measure:
She looked down into the *fathomless* canyon.

deny *v.* to refuse to give or grant:
No one can *deny* her the right to speak.
reject to refuse to accept, believe, or grant:
He may *reject* the job offer.
refuse to withhold acceptance of; turn down:

I don't know anyone who would *refuse* a
million dollars.

decline to refuse politely:
I'm sorry, but I must *decline* the invitation
to the party.

rebuff to reject bluntly or rudely:
Don't *rebuff* your friend's offer to help.

depend *v.* to count on:
I can *depend* on my sister.

rely to trust in:
I will *rely* on you to be on time.

trust to have confidence in:
You can *trust* me to walk the dog twice
a day.

describe *v.* to give a picture in words; to tell
or write about:
In my letter, I will *describe* the buildings of
Savannah to my friends back home.

portray to describe:
When he writes stories, Victor likes to
portray his main characters as brave and
adventurous.

depict to represent in words.
Hassan's magazine article will *depict* the
old house his grandparents built.

paint to describe vividly in words:
My aunt's old letters *paint* a humorous
picture of her life.

deserve *v.* to have a right to:
The students *deserve* extra recess time for
their hard work this morning.

earn to win because of hard work or good
behavior:

Chris will *earn* extra credit points if he completes his social studies assignment.

merit to be worthy of:

I hope the book report I just handed in will be good enough to *merit* a high grade.

dirt *n.* earth:

He slid through the *dirt* to reach third base safely.

soil the dirt that is the top part of the ground:

We planted seeds in the *soil* in our yard.

ground the part of the earth that is solid:

Apples fell from the tree to the *ground*.

mud wet dirt:

After it rained, there was *mud* everywhere.

disappear *v.* to go out of sight:

The jet will soon *disappear* into the clouds.

vanish to go out of sight or existence:

When you use this cleaner, stains will *vanish*.

fade to become fainter and disappear:

We heard the fire engines' sirens *fade* into the distance.

evaporate to fade away or end:

Your home run caused the other team's hopes for a win to *evaporate*.

disappoint *v.* to fail to live up to a wish or hope:

Rainy weather at the game on Saturday will *disappoint* the soccer team.

let down not to do as expected by others:

By not showing up for the game, Shirley *let down* the team.

dissatisfy to fail to meet a need or wish:
You *dissatisfy* me when you break a
promise.

discussion *n.* the act of talking something
over, often to exchange ideas:
Before doing the spelling exercises, we
had a *discussion* about word endings.
talk an exchange of spoken words:
My uncle said he wanted to have a *talk*
with me about our vacation plans.
conversation talk between two or more
people:
They interrupted their *conversation* to
give their tickets to the conductor.
chat a friendly, informal talk:
Margarita hoped to have a *chat* with her
friends before the basketball game started.

dismiss *v.* to send away or allow to leave:
The coach will *dismiss* the team members
as soon as practice ends.
discharge to let go or clear out:
The team leader will *discharge* the
volunteers as soon as their job is done.
excuse to release from duty or attendance:
Because of the blizzard, the principal
plans to *excuse* the students early so they
can get home safely.

dive *v.* to make a sudden downward
movement:
One by one, the swimmers *dive* into the
pool.
plunge to fall suddenly:
Did you see the kite *plunge* to the ground?

swoop to rush down suddenly:
Look at the hawk *swoop* down on the rabbit.

dot *n.* a small, round mark usually made for a purpose:
The map has a *dot* on it to show where the city is.

point a dot used in math:
The cents *point* in $2.69 shows that this amount is two dollars and sixty-nine cents.

speck a small mark that can be any shape:
You left a *speck* of paint on the desk.

spot a mark that can be any size or shape:
My gray cat has a white *spot* on her chest.

drag *v.* to move something along slowly or heavily:
The horse strained to *drag* the overloaded hay wagon.

haul to pull or move with effort:
The day we moved into the new house, it took three people to *haul* the file cabinet up the stairs.

tow to pull or drag behind:
I can hardly believe that this little truck will be able to *tow* the school bus out of the ditch.

dull *adj.* not interesting:
They walked out of the *dull* movie before it was over.

boring lacking in interest:
I almost fell asleep because the TV program was so *boring*.

tiresome causing boredom or weariness:
　　Mrs. Rodriguez said that she didn't want
　　to hear any more of our *tiresome* excuses.
tedious long and tiring, boring:
　　Checking all the addresses was a
　　tedious task.

easily *adv.* without difficulty or effort:
　　Our team *easily* won the game.
smoothly free from obstacles or difficulties:
　　The ship passed *smoothly* through the
　　rough water.
handily in a handy or easy way:
　　His wheelchair *handily* passed through the
　　doorway.
effortlessly without effort or difficulty:
　　The pianist seemed to play *effortlessly*.

easy *adj.* not hard or difficult:
　　It was an *easy* lesson.
simple without problem:
　　A sandwich is a *simple* snack to make.
effortless using no effort or strain:
　　Good athletes make winning look
　　effortless.

edge *n.* the part where something ends:
　　The ball rolled off the *edge* of the table.
rim the outer part of something round or
curved:
　　The *rim* of the plate was painted gold.
border the outer part or edge:
　　The *border* of the skirt has yellow lace
　　along it.

side the part farthest from the center:
I drew cars along the left *side* of my picture.

effect *n.* something brought about by a cause or agent:
One *effect* of the rain was that the grass began to turn from brown to green.
result something brought about by an action, process, or condition:
As a *result* of the election, he became president.
consequence something that results from an earlier action:
As a *consequence* of not studying, she did not do well on the test.
outcome a result or consequence:
The damaged trees are an *outcome* of the hurricane.

employ *v.* to pay someone to do a job:
Our neighbor will *employ* Rita to rake the leaves.
hire to give a job to:
If you *hire* me, I'll do a good job.
engage to hire:
I will *engage* a secretary to take notes at the meeting.
appoint to name for a job or an office:
The President can *appoint* certain judges.

enclose *v.* to close in on all sides:
We may *enclose* the yard with a fence.
surround to be on all sides of:
The fans *surround* the actress.
encircle to form a circle around:
In the game, the children *encircle*

someone who is "it."

encompass to form a circle around:

The wall will *encompass* the entire garden.

ring to put a ring around; enclose with
a ring:

The gravel path will *ring* the cottage.

enjoyable *adj.* giving joy or happiness:

The children spent an *enjoyable* afternoon
at the beach.

pleasant giving a feeling of happiness:

It is *pleasant* to sit in the shade on a hot
day.

agreeable nice, to one's liking:

The good weather made our trip to the
beach most *agreeable*.

enjoyment *n.* a happy or pleased feeling:

Baseball gives me much *enjoyment*.

pleasure a satisfied or pleased feeling:

Pleasure can come from a job well done.

delight joy:

It is a *delight* to listen to good music.

happiness gladness:

Matthew got much *happiness* from the
surprise party.

entertainment *n.* something that interests
and amuses:

After working all day, we went to a
concert for *entertainment*.

fun enjoyment:

Just for *fun*, let's go down to the canal and
watch the barges.

recreation something that is done for
relaxation or amusement:

Sports are a kind of *recreation*.

equal *adj.* the same in size, amount, or value:
Five pennies are *equal* to one nickel.
even the same:
   At the end of the fifth inning the score in
   the game was *even*.
matching the same, for example in size, color,
or shape:
   The sisters wore *matching* hats.
similar almost the same:
   The two cars are *similar* but not
   exactly alike.

errands *n.* pl. of errand. things that a person is
sent to do:
   Monday I will run some *errands* at the
   store for my mom.
tasks jobs that must be done:
   Luis gave Ned some *tasks* to do
   downtown.
missions special jobs or tasks:
   The president sent people to several
   countries on *missions* of peace.

especially *adv.* mostly:
   They *especially* wanted to see the Statue
   of Liberty when they visited New York.
particularly to a great degree, a lot:
   The teacher was *particularly* pleased with
   our report on hurricanes.
chiefly above all, mainly:
   The cat was *chiefly* interested in who was
   going to feed her.
primarily for the most part, most importantly:
   The crossing guard is *primarily*
   responsible for making sure the children
   cross safely.

exact *adj.* very accurate:

Do you need an *exact* answer for this addition problem, or is a rounded answer close enough?

precise very accurate or definite:

The captain's *precise* directions led us to the treasure.

correct free from error:

The recipe gave the *correct* amounts for all the ingredients.

accurate making few or no errors or mistakes:

Most of her answers on the test were *accurate*.

---

exciting *adj.* causing stirred-up, strong feelings.

bracing	rousing
breathtaking	sensational
fascinating	stirring
interesting	thrilling
moving	

- antonyms: dull, boring, flat

---

explore *v.* to look through closely:

The class will begin to *explore* the history of space travel next week.

investigate to look into carefully in order to get information:

Each group will *investigate* a different animal that lives in the desert.

study to try to learn about:

Next year we will *study* geometry and world history.

research to study carefully in order to find facts; to investigate:

My sister went to the public library in order to *research* our family tree.

faith *n.* a feeling that something is true, or can be counted on:

The city of Montreal was unfamiliar to the travelers, but they had *faith* in the accuracy of their guidebook.

belief an acceptance of something as true:

Mrs. Ruiz has a strong *belief* that every one of her students can do excellent work.

trust a belief that something can be counted on:

My neighbor has *trust* in my ability to baby-sit her children.

confidence a feeling that something can be relied on:

I have *confidence* in my ability to finish the assignment before the deadline.

fasten *v.* to put two things together firmly:

We used a bolt to *fasten* the tire swing to the chain.

connect to join together:

The driver had to back up in order to *connect* the trailer to the car.

attach to connect one thing to another:

They used glue to *attach* the badges to the notebooks.

bind to tie or join together:

When we finish our stories, the teacher will *bind* them into a class book.

favor *n.* a generous or kind act:

As a *favor,* she lent me a book.

courtesy an act of good manners:

Lou did me the *courtesy* of letting me use his umbrella.

kindness a kind or thoughtful act:

As a *kindness* to me, please turn your radio down.

fear *n.* a feeling that trouble or danger is near:

He has a *fear* of heights.

fright a sudden, strong feeling of danger:

Surprising me like that gave me a real *fright.*

scare a sudden panic:

We jumped out and gave them a *scare.*

terror a great feeling of danger:

The *terror* in the movie was caused by dinosaurs.

fight *v.* to have a big disagreement:

It's silly to *fight* over what game we should play.

disagree to have different opinions, in either a calm or angry way:

We always *disagree* about what TV show to watch.

argue to disagree in words, in either a calm or angry way:

You don't have to yell at people when you *argue.*

quarrel to have angry words with each other:

When they *quarrel,* one of them always stomps off angrily.

final *adj.* coming at the end:
    I read the *final* chapter of the book.
last at the end, after all the others:
    The *last* runner reached the finish line.
concluding bringing a thing or series to
an end:
    He made the *concluding* speech of the
    play, and the curtain fell.
closing bringing something to an end:
    After the chorus sang its *closing* song, the
    program ended.

finish *v.* to bring or come to an end:
    Tom wants to *finish* his picture this
    afternoon.
conclude to finish:
    We will *conclude* the show by singing
    a song.
complete to bring to an end by doing the
whole thing:
    To *complete* this test, you must answer ten
    questions.
stop to keep from continuing:
    Stop making that noise, and play quietly.

flare *n.* a sudden bright light, especially one
that lasts for only a short time.
    Jay saw a *flare* of light in the dark sky.
blaze a bright, intense light:
    The spotlights all came on at once,
    creating a *blaze* of brilliant white light.
flash a sudden, short burst of light:
    I saw a *flash* of lightning about five
    seconds before I heard the thunder roll.
glare a strong, usually unpleasant light:
    In the *glare* of the sun, even the sidewalks
    seemed to shrivel up.

flash *n.* a sudden burst of light:

A *flash* of lightning lit the sky for a second.

gleam a beam of light:

I could see the *gleam* of a flashlight in the darkness.

sparkle a glittering light:

The *sparkle* of sunlight on the water was beautiful.

twinkle a winking light:

Streetlights shine steadily, but stars give off a *twinkle*.

flaw *n.* something that spoils or takes away from perfection or completeness:

There is a *flaw* in the leather of those boots.

defect an imperfection or weakness:

A *defect* in the software kept the computer from running.

imperfection not perfect; having a flaw.

The jewel was on sale because it had a slight *imperfection*.

shortcoming a fault or defect:

Carelessness is a serious *shortcoming*.

fled *v.* past tense and past participle of flee. to have run away:

We *fled* before the hurricane arrived.

escaped got away or got free:

Once again our cat *escaped* from the house.

took flight left quickly:

The crowd *took flight* when the ground began to shake.

bolted made a sudden spring or start:

The antelope *bolted* when it saw the lion.

foam *n.* a mass of tiny bubbles:

If you add vinegar to baking soda, the mixture will produce *foam*.

froth bubbles formed in or on a liquid:

The *froth* in the milkshake comes from the shaking.

lather bubbles formed by mixing soap and water:

Work up a good *lather* with shampoo to get your hair really clean.

suds soap bubbles:

I was up to my elbows in *suds* from the dishes when the phone rang.

---

foolish *adj.* showing a lack of understanding or good sense.

absurd	nonsensical
frivolous	ridiculous
irrational	silly
laughable	unwise
ludicrous	

- antonyms: wise, intelligent, smart

---

force *v.* to make someone do something:

Don't *force* Yuka to go if she doesn't want to.

compel to force:

The storm will *compel* us to cancel the game.

coerce to make someone act in a given manner:

The bully tried to *coerce* the children to walk on the other side of the street.

require to demand in a way that can't be refused:

A police officer can *require* cars to stop even when the light is green.

frequent *adj.* taking place again and again:

He is a *frequent* guest at our house.

repeated done or happening again and again:

They have made *repeated* visits to the town.

continual happening over and over again without stop:

Continual dry weather caused the crops to fail.

constant continuing without a break:

The *constant* noise kept me awake all night.

numerous forming a large number; many:

The phone rang *numerous* times.

friends *n,* pl. of friend. people one likes:

All of my *friends* came to my birthday party.

pals friends:

My *pals* and I play ball together almost every day.

buddies friends:

He and his *buddies* enjoyed the day off together.

frighten *v.* to make suddenly alarmed or scared:

Spiders *frighten* me.

alarm to cause to feel sudden fear:

Did the loud noise *alarm* you?

horrify to cause to feel horror:

The sight of a snake can *horrify* some people.

terrify to frighten or alarm greatly:
  The silly ghost story did not *terrify* me.
petrify to paralyze with fear:
  A dog's loud growl can *petrify* some cats,
  but my cat just growls back.

frown *v.* to express anger or sadness with a
look on the face:
  Mom will *frown* when she sees the mess
  our dog made.
glare to give an angry look:
  A messy room will make him *glare* in
  anger.
scowl to look at in a displeased way:
  The barking dog caused Lucy to *scowl*.

frozen *Adjective,* formed from the past
participle of the verb freeze. made or
become so cold that ice has formed in or
on it:
  No seeds could be planted in the hard,
  frozen ground.
icy made of or covered with ice:
  The sidewalk was *icy* after the storm.
frosty cold enough for ice to form; freezing:
  The *frosty* air made me wish I had gloves
  on.

furious *adj.* extremely mad:
  Losing her wallet made Bess *furious*.
angry feeling or showing anger:
  The *angry* child stamped her feet and
  screamed.
enraged very angry:
  The bear becomes *enraged* when anyone
  gets close to her cub.

gain *v.* to get through work or effort:
> If she sticks with her training program, Shaniqua will *gain* skill and strength.

achieve to do or reach successfully:
> Next year, Carlos will *achieve* his goal of becoming a pilot.

attain to achieve or gain through work or effort:
> Some people *attain* stardom through hard work and good luck.

garbage *n.* unwanted things that are thrown out:
> Much of the *garbage* in our house comes from the packaging around food.

trash unwanted things that are thrown out:
> Bottles should be recycled and not thrown away as *trash*.

rubbish useless material that is or should be thrown away:
> He threw away the torn, crumpled papers and other *rubbish*.

refuse things that are thrown out:
> The *refuse* will be taken out to the curb in the morning.

gentle *adj.* mild and kind; not rough:
> Babies need *gentle* handling.

soft smooth to the touch; not hard or sharp:
> A *soft* breeze is blowing across the field.

tender delicate; kind or loving:
> When I am sick, I need *tender* care.

gigantic *adj.* very big and powerful, like a giant.

colossal   monumental
enormous   mountainous
huge   towering
immense   tremendous
mammoth   vast

■ antonyms: tiny, minute, microscopic

give *v.* to hand over.
     I will *give* Dave two tickets to the game.
     present to give:
         Our parents will *present* the family's gift to Grandma.
     pass to hand or move something to another person:
         Please *pass* me the milk.
     offer to present something that could be either taken or turned down:
         I will *offer* the guests cake.
     surrender to give something up:
         When the other team captured all of our players, we had to *surrender* our flag.

glare *n.* a strong, unpleasant light:
     He shaded his eyes against the spotlight's *glare*.
     blaze a strong light:
         The *blaze* of the sun made us want to walk on the shady side of the street.
     flash a sudden, short burst of light:
         I saw a *flash* of lightning near the hills.
     flare a sudden bright light:
         We saw the *flare* of fireworks in the night sky.

goal *n.* something that a person wants to get or become:

My *goal* is to be able to spell any word I hear.

objective a desired end result:

The *objective* of the game is to collect as many pieces as possible.

purpose the reason for which something exists or is done:

What is the *purpose* of the new machine?

aim the point toward which an action is directed:

His *aim* was to run a marathon in under three hours.

goes *v.* present tense of go. moves from one point to another:

This bus *goes* from the town hall to the library.

moves changes place or position:

That robot *moves* its arms and legs.

proceeds moves onward:

At that point, the song *proceeds* at a slower beat.

continues keeps moving in the same direction:

The horse *continues* along the road at a gallop.

grab *v.* to take hold of suddenly and with force:

The baby will try to *grab* your glasses.

snatch to grab:

Did the dog *snatch* the bone right out of your hand?

seize to take hold of with force:
> Our team will *seize* the ball and run down the field.

clutch to hold tightly:
> The baby will *clutch* his teddy bear until he falls asleep.

grip to hold tightly:
> If you *grip* the rail, you won't slip.

grand *adj.* large and wonderful to look at:
> The town built a *grand* tower to mark its hundredth year.

splendid showy and grand:
> When the curtain rises, you'll see a *splendid* palace onstage.

magnificent wonderful to look at and often rich-looking:
> A *magnificent* golden mirror hung on the wall.

glorious stirring or beautiful to look at:
> A *glorious* sunrise filled the sky

grateful *adj.* full of warm feelings for something that makes one happy or comfortable:
> They were *grateful* to find shelter from the rain.

thankful feeling aware of receiving a favor or benefit:
> The new students were *thankful* for the advice of their classmates.

appreciative showing or feeling thankfulness:
> The *appreciative* audience stood up and cheered.

group *n.* two or more people or things together.

batch	gathering
bunch	heap
club	mass
collection	pile
crew	stack
crowd	team

■antonym: individual

grown-up *adj.* characteristic of adults:
The child tried to speak in a *grown-up* way.
adult relating to or for adults:
At dinner, the children were expected to behave in an *adult* manner.
mature showing characteristics of a fully grown person:
The young baseball player had a *mature* approach to fame.
seasoned made suitable for use by experience and age:
He was a *seasoned* city official.

guess *v.* to form an opinion without enough information:
I *guess* there are six hundred marbles in that jar.
estimate to form an opinion of the value or cost of something:
I *estimate* it will cost $50.00 to repair the bike.
suppose to believe that something is possible but not certain:
I *suppose* Jean will lend you her scarf.

hamper *v.* to interfere with the action or progress of:

> The runner's sore leg will *hamper* him in the race.

impede to get in the way of or to delay:

> We are eager to start our trip, and we hope the storm won't *impede* us.

interfere with to cause an interruption or hindrance:

> The cold weather did not *interfere with* our plans to go swimming.

hinder to delay or make difficult the movement or progress of:

> The fog could *hinder* the arrival of the plane.

happily *adv.* with pleasure or joy:

> They *happily* ate the delicious food.

blissfully full of great happiness or joy:

> Mei Lee *blissfully* hugged her newly found cat.

blithely full of joy or cheer:

> The skater *blithely* skimmed across the ice.

merrily in a joyous or merry manner:

> The children *merrily* sang holiday songs.

cheerfully full of cheer; in a good-tempered manner:

> Jed *cheerfully* volunteered to help with the party.

harm *v.* to cause someone or something injury or problems:

>You can *harm* a plant by not giving it water.

hurt to give pain to:

>If you fight you will *hurt* each other.

damage to harm or make less valuable:

>Carelessness can cause *damage* to property.

injure to hurt:

>Rose wears a helmet so she will not *injure* herself when she rides her bike.

harmful *adj.* causing loss or pain:

>The older children made sure to keep *harmful* things out of the baby's reach.

hurtful causing pain:

>Hassan apologized for the *hurtful* things he had said.

destructive causing or bringing injury or harm:

>The *destructive* winds of the hurricane broke windows and knocked down trees.

haul *v.* to move a heavy object:

>The oxen will *haul* the cart.

pull to grab and move toward oneself:

>The wheels on a wagon make it easy to *pull* even if it is loaded with groceries.

drag to move something along slowly:

>*Drag* the couch over near the fireplace.

tug to pull on something with great energy:

>If you *tug* hard, the stuck door will open.

heap *n.* a collection of things piled together:
A *heap* of dirty clothes lay beside the washer.

pile a number of things laid or lying on one another:
Somewhere in this *pile* of socks, there must be a matching pair.

stack a pile of things arranged in an orderly way:
The *stack* of books lay on the night table.

mass a large quantity, amount, or number:
A *mass* of money was stacked inside the huge vault.

hesitate *v.* to wait or stop a moment:
If you *hesitate* before swinging at the ball, you may miss it.

pause to stop for a short time:
The marching band will *pause* before the reviewing stand before continuing down the parade route.

delay to put off or slow down action:
People who *delay* when faced with a decision might end up with fewer choices.

falter to act with hesitation or uncertainty:
People who rehearse their parts well are less likely to get nervous and *falter* midway through a speech.

hid *v.* past tense of hide. put out of sight:
I *hid* the presents in the closet.

concealed hid:
The children *concealed* themselves behind the curtain.

secreted hid:

He *secreted* the jewels somewhere in those caves.

covered was in front of something so that the thing was out of sight:

The cloud *covered* the moon.

veiled covered something with a cloth so it was hard to see:

She *veiled* her face so she wouldn't be recognized.

hidden *Adjective,* formed from the past participle of the verb hide. put or kept out of sight:

Sean searched for hours before he found the *hidden* lizard in the picture.

concealed kept out of sight:

Margo's fingers felt the *concealed* lock even though it was almost impossible to see.

secret known only to oneself or a few:

George and Margie looked for hours until they finally found the papers in a *secret* drawer in the old desk.

hoist *v.* to pull up:

The movers used a rope and a pulley to *hoist* the piano into the van.

raise to put in a higher position:

Olivia tried to *raise* the window in order to let some air into the stuffy room.

lift to move from a lower to a higher position:

Let's *lift* the lid so that we can see what's inside the treasure chest.

honor *v.* to treat with great respect:
  We have a holiday to *honor* our war
  veterans.

praise to speak well of someone or
something:
  Speakers will *praise* the winner of the
  medal.

esteem to think highly of:
  We *esteem* teachers for their knowledge.

admire to feel great respect for:
  I *admire* the tired runner for finishing
  the race.

cheer to give a shout of praise:
  We *cheer* our heroes to show them our
  respect.

---

horde *n.* a large group.

bevy	mob
crowd	multitude
drove	myriads
flock	pack
gathering	swarm
mass	throng

---

howl *n.* a loud, wailing cry.

bellow	screech
shriek	wail
scream	yell
shout	yowl

■antonyms: whisper, murmur

huge *adj.* extremely big.

enormous	monstrous
giant	sizable
gigantic	towering
great	tremendous
jumbo	vast
mammoth	whopping
massive	

- antonyms: tiny, small, little

hurry *n.* the act of moving quickly:

He ran down the hall because he was in a *hurry.*

rush a quick movement:

He spoke slowly at first, but he finished his speech in a *rush.*

haste a hurry:

If you do your homework in great *haste,* it will be full of mistakes.

dash a fast movement:

The children made a *dash* toward the door when the bell rang.

bustle movement that is quick and full of energy:

The kitchen was full of *bustle* and noise just before lunch.

imagine *v.* to picture something in one's mind:

The teacher asked the children to *imagine* what it would be like to live in another time in history.

suppose to think about something as if it is possible or really happening:

    Suppose you had the chance to go to the Olympics.

guess to form an opinion without having enough knowledge or facts to be sure:

    Harold couldn't *guess* the writer of that story.

immediately *adv.* done or happening without delay:

    The ambulance went *immediately* to the hospital.

at once immediately; without delay:

    When the storm began, we closed the windows *at once*.

promptly done or given without delay:

    She answered his letter *promptly*.

readily quickly or promptly:

    He answered my questions *readily*, without hesitating.

instantly without delay:

    I recognized his face *instantly*.

impolite *adj.* not having or showing good manners:

    The *impolite* remark made him angry.

rude not polite or courteous:

    Such *rude* behavior deserved to be punished.

disrespectful rude or impolite:

    Disrespectful audiences sometimes boo loudly.

discourteous not courteous; not polite:

A *discourteous* tone of voice can offend
people even if the actual words you say
are not rude.

important *adj.* having great value or meaning:
Education is very *important*.
significant having special value or meaning:
July 4th is a *significant* day in American
history.
major chief or more important:
The *major* reason I jog is to relax.

inactive *adj.* not active; not full of activity:
Many desert animals are *inactive* during
the day when temperatures soar.
sluggish showing little activity:
Our pace was *sluggish* because we were
tired.
languid showing a lack of energy or force:
He answered slowly with a sleepy, *languid*
voice.
lethargic sluggish:
Their *lethargic* singing almost caused me
to fall asleep.
listless lacking energy or desire to do
anything:
Joaquin's *listless* walk showed his
disappointment.

independence *n.* the ability to govern oneself
or make one's own decisions:
A job gives people *independence* because
they don't need to count on others to fill
their basic needs.
freedom the state of not being under the
control of others:

The citizens of our country value the *freedom* to live where and how they please.

liberty political independence; the state of being free from the control of a harsh government:

Britain was forced to grant *liberty* to the American colonists.

informal *adj.* not formal, without ceremony or following any rigid form:

The mayor agreed to an *informal* interview with the class.

casual not formal:

We were told to wear *casual* clothes to the party.

relaxed less strict, not rigid or tense:

The *relaxed* surroundings of the playroom helped the shy child get used to her new friends.

insert *v.* to put something into:

Insert your card into the slot.

enter to put in or on:

Ms. Cheng will *enter* our names on the list for the award.

enclose to put something in along with something else:

He will *enclose* a check in the envelope with his letter.

inside *n.* the inner part:

The *inside* of an egg is soft and liquid.

interior the inside:

The *interior* of the house was cool.
core the central part:

The *core* of the earth is made of super-hot, melted iron.
heart the center:

All the paths meet at the *heart* of the maze.

instrument *n.* a tool used for precise or careful work:

A telescope is an *instrument* for observing distant objects.
tool something used for doing work:

A hammer is a *tool* for driving nails into wood.
device something made for a particular purpose:

A screen saver is a *device* to keep a computer screen from burning out.
implement something used in performing a task or other work:

The sculptor used a long, thin *implement* to carve the mouth and the eyes.
mechanism an instrument used for doing something:

A clock is a *mechanism* for keeping track of time.

jealous *adj.* wanting what someone else has:

Don't be *jealous* of a friend's popularity.
envious feeling jealousy:

He felt *envious* once he saw John's new bike.
competitive always trying to compete with

or get the better of other people:

Lee is so *competitive* that he can't even stand it when people get ahead of him on the lunch line.

jewel *n.* a valuable stone such as a diamond:

The ring had a glittering *jewel* set into a gold band.

gem a stone of great value:

The story was about a lost *gem* that belonged to a prince.

precious stone the most valuable kind of jewel, usually a diamond, ruby, emerald, or sapphire:

A *precious stone* can be cut and polished so that it glitters.

treasure something of great value, such as gold or a jewel:

The hidden *treasure* will be found as soon as we can figure out the code used on this map.

join *v.* to put things together so they become like one:

You can *join* the two ends of a rope by tying a knot.

connect to put things together:

You need to *connect* the paper clips to make a chain.

attach to put things together so they don't come apart:

Use glue to *attach* the cutouts to the collage.

fasten to attach firmly:

Use a safety pin to *fasten* your name tag to your shirt.

jolly *adj.* cheerful:
>The *jolly* children laughed and joked as they skipped along.

merry jolly:
>The radio played a *merry* tune that made me want to dance.

happy in a good mood:
>I always feel *happy* on sunny, warm days.

glad happy, usually about something special:
>I am *glad* that my team won the game.

journal *n.* a record, especially one kept daily, of events, experiences, or thoughts:
>Juan writes in his *journal* every evening.

diary a daily record of events, especially of the writer's personal experiences and thoughts:
>Keiko writes her *diary* on her word processor.

log any record of progress, performance, or events:
>The explorers kept a *log* of what happened during their sea voyage.

journey *n.* a long trip:
>They wrote postcards from every stop on their *journey*.

trip the act of going from one place to another:
>The class will take a *trip* to the state park.

expedition a long trip made for a specific reason:
>The scientists will collect mosses on their *expedition* to the northern plains.

trek a long trip, especially when slow or difficult:

We were on the road for days, and sometimes it seemed as if our *trek* would never end.

excursion a short trip made for a specific reason:

The bus left in the morning for the *excursion* to the zoo.

joy *n.* a happy feeling:

That piece of music always fills me with *joy*.

happiness the feeling of being happy or pleased:

Winning the race filled her with *happiness*.

delight pleasure or enjoyment:

Traveling to new places gives me great *delight*.

jump *v.* to use one's legs to push oneself up into the air:

He had to *jump* to catch the ball.

leap to make a long or high jump:

I tried to *leap* across the puddle, but I didn't make it.

spring to move upward or forward quickly:

My cat will *spring* at a mouse as soon as she sees it.

hop to make a short jump on one foot:

In hopscotch, players *hop* from square to square.

skip to jump from one foot to the other:

The children *skip* to the rhythm of the music.

keen *adj.* very sensitive or acute:

Deborah has a *keen* sense of fashion.

sharp having the ability to perceive or feel quickly:

His *sharp* ears recognized the disguised voice.

acute very sensitive; keen:

Her *acute* sense of touch helped her find the key in the dark.

fine sharp; keen:

Great cooks usually have a *fine* sense of smell.

kept *v.* past tense of keep. had or held onto:

Jenny *kept* the game-winning ball.

saved put aside or held onto:

I *saved* all the postcards that my uncle sent me.

owned had as a belonging:

He *owned* a car, but he never drove it.

held had in one's hands:

He *held* the kitten carefully.

kernel *n.* the central, most valuable or most important part:

The first paragraph of a newspaper report often presents the *kernel* of the report.

gist a main idea or central point:

Read the television listing to find out the *gist* of the new show.

essence a necessary and basic part:

The *essence* of the plot is a missing jewel.

substance the real or essential thing or part, especially of something written or spoken:
> The *substance* of the chapter was a discussion of how to use a thesaurus.

knew *v.* past tense of know. was certain of the facts about something:
> I *knew* the names of all fifty states.

understood was aware of the meaning or importance of something:
> I *understood* why I had to multiply to solve that problem.

grasped saw or got the meaning of:
> After much work he *grasped* the idea.

knife *n.* a cutting tool with a blade attached to a handle:
> Be careful not to cut yourself when using a *knife*.

scalpel a small, straight knife with a thin blade:
> A doctor uses a *scalpel* to operate.

dagger a small weapon that looks like a knife:
> The characters in the story I am reading found a *dagger* in the cave they were exploring.

knock *v.* to hit sharply and hard:
> Please *knock* on the door before you come in.

rap to hit sharply and hard:
> Did you *rap* on the door, or did you ring the bell?

tap to hit lightly and quickly:

Tap your fingers against the window to get her attention.

pound to hit very hard:

Use the hammer to *pound* the nail into the wood.

punch to press hard or quickly with one's fist or finger:

Would you *punch* the elevator button for me?

knowledge *n.* what is known from experience, study, or awareness:

Carlos has a vast *knowledge* of history.

understanding thorough knowledge or mastery:

Mrs. Burke's *understanding* of computers helped her become familiar with the Internet.

acquaintance knowledge of something, especially as a result of personal experience or contact:

Randy's years of living in Montreal gave him a thorough *acquaintance* with the French language.

known *v.* past participle of know. to have been certain of the facts or truth of:

I have *known* that story since I was a little child.

understood to have known very well:

We have *understood* our responsibility from the first day we started this job.

recognized to have accepted that something is true:

Doctors have always *recognized* the importance of eating fresh vegetables.

labor *n.* hard work:

After the cement was poured, the workers could rest from their *labor*.

work the use of a person's energy or ability to do something:

We have a lot of *work* to do on our science project.

toil hard or exhausting work:

The *toil* of digging up the ground makes starting a garden a difficult job.

effort hard work:

When the rain started, they were glad they had put the *effort* into finishing the roof.

---

laugh *v.* to show a happy feeling by making a sound.

chuckle	**roar**
giggle	**shriek**
guffaw	**snicker**
howl	**snort**

- antonyms: mope, sob, moan, groan

---

lay *v.* to put:

I will *lay* my gloves on this shelf.

set to put:

Please *set* the bowl carefully on the table so it doesn't spill.

place to put in a particular spot:

Place the cake in the center of the table.

rest to set down:

You can *rest* the books on that table.

leader *n.* a person who shows the way:

The scout *leader* showed the troop how to follow the animal tracks to the stream.

guide a person who shows the way:

The *guide* led the children out of the forest.

director a person who supervises or guides other people:

The *director* of the tour pointed out the sights in the city.

learn *v.* to get to know through study or practice:

Did you *learn* how to draw at school?

discover to see something for the first time:

How did you *discover* the answer?

realize to become aware:

Do you *realize* how lucky you are?

leave *v.* to move off or away from a place:

The birds will *leave* this lake and fly south for the winter.

go to leave:

I can stay here all afternoon, but I have to *go* before it gets dark.

depart to go away:
> The plane will *depart* from the airport at noon.

exit to go out, usually from a room or a building:
> You must *exit* the school by the side door.

set out to leave in order to begin a trip:
> The family *set out* for their hike.

lid *n.* a cover that can be put on or off:
> Put the *lid* on the box so dust doesn't collect inside.

cover something that is put on something else:
> The pan has a *cover* to keep the food warm.

top a cover or lid:
> The jar has a *top* that can be screwed back on.

cap a close-fitting cover, usually of a bottle:
> You need a bottle opener to remove the *cap* from this juice bottle.

limit *v.* to keep within bounds:
> The rules *limit* each speaker to five minutes.

restrict to keep within specified limits:
> The plaster cast will *restrict* the movement of her hand.

confine to keep within limits; restrict:
> The fence will *confine* the dog to our yard.

narrow to make smaller in width or extent:
> You need to *narrow* the topic of your paper.

listen *v.* to try to hear; pay attention:
> *Listen* when the teacher is speaking.

hear to receive sound through the ears:
> Do you *hear* what I'm saying?

heed to pay careful attention to; listen or mind:
> I will *heed* my parent's advice and wear a sweater to the ball game.

locate *v.* to discover the exact place of:
> I can't *locate* the town on this map.

pinpoint to find precisely:
> The building plan will help you *pinpoint* the location of each window.

find to discover the location of:
> You will *find* a pencil in the desk drawer.

spot to pick out by sight:
> The binoculars will help you *spot* the nest in the tree.

loiter *v.* to move slowly or with frequent pauses:
> Tourists often *loiter* along the paths of the ancient ruined city.

linger to go or act at a slow pace:
> We decided to *linger* on the way to the museum so that we could see the sidewalk art show.

dawdle to waste time; linger:
> My young sisters often *dawdle* as they walk home.

dillydally to waste time:
> Those students don't *dillydally* after school but instead go straight home.

loom *v.* to appear as a large, menacing shape:
  The huge trees *loom* over the tiny house.
threaten to hang over dangerously; to loom:
  Heavy dark clouds *threaten* on the horizon.
overshadow to cast a shadow over, as a larger
object does to a smaller one:
  The giant office towers *overshadow* the
  three-story apartment building squeezed
  between them.
hover to remain suspended in the air over a
particular spot or object:
  The giant blimps *hover* over the field.

loud *adj.* making a strong sound:
  The *loud* radio made it too hard to read.
noisy making a strong sound:
  Children can be *noisy* at recess.
blaring creating a strong, unpleasant noise:
  The fire truck has a *blaring* siren.

love *v.* to have a strong, warm feeling for:
  I *love* my pets very much.
adore to love greatly:
  The children *adore* their grandparents.
enjoy to get joy or pleasure from; be
happy with:
  I *enjoy* the company of my sisters.

loyal *adj.* faithful to a person, cause, or ideal:
  Washington's soldiers were *loyal* to him.
true faithful:
  Jerry proved he was a *true* friend when he
  protected Dave from some bullies.
trusty capable of being trusted or relied on:
  My *trusty* watch never failed me.

loyalty *n.* strong and lasting faithfulness and support:

My sister showed her *loyalty* by going to all my soccer games.

devotion a strong affection or great faithfulness:

The volunteer's *devotion* to the cause was shown by his tireless work.

steadfastness firm and devoted loyalty:

We proved our *steadfastness* by cheering even when our team was losing.

lure *v.* to attract strongly:

We hoped the seeds on the floor would *lure* the gerbil out from behind the bookcase.

attract to cause to come near:

If you don't want flies, you shouldn't leave out food that will *attract* them.

tempt to appeal strongly to:

The offer of a free sample was enough to *tempt* many people into the store.

draw to cause to move toward, to attract:

The clowns made lots of noise to *draw* a crowd.

lying *v.* present participle of lie. stretching out:

It is easier to fall asleep *lying* down than sitting up.

reclining leaning back; lying down:

Jake is *reclining* on the sofa and reading a book.

sprawling lying or sitting with the body stretched out in an awkward or careless manner:

My dog spent the morning *sprawling* on the rug with his eyes closed.

major *adj.* greater than others in importance or rank.

dominant   leading
greater   primary
higher   ranking
key   superior

■ antonyms: minor, unimportant, insignificant

maneuver *v.* to use skillful or clever moves or plans:

His the driver had to *maneuver* her car carefully on the icy roadway.

plot to form a plan or scheme:

His friends will *plot* to surprise him on his birthday.

scheme to make a plan; plot:

Sherlock Holmes will often *scheme* to catch a villain.

devise to plan or think out:

Officials should *devise* a more efficient public transportation system.

concoct to put together; devise:

You always *concoct* such funny stories!

manufacture *v.* to make or process something, especially using machinery:

We visited a big building where they *manufacture* bicycles.

produce to make or create something:

The workers in the garment factory *produce* a complete shirt every fifteen minutes.

assemble to make something by putting parts together:

Workers in the Michigan plant *assemble* car parts that were produced in Canada.

march *v.* to walk with regular steps as soldiers do:

The children will *march* into the stadium in two straight lines.

tramp to walk or step heavily:

The band members *tramp* along in time to the music.

parade to march in a parade:

The teams will *parade* past the cheering crowds.

step to lift each foot and put it down in another place.

Step in time to the music as you walk.

---

mark *n.* a spot or scar made by one thing or another, by accident or on purpose.

line	spot
scratch	streak
smudge	stroke

marshal *v.* to arrange in proper or logical order:

> To write the paper, he will *marshal* information from several sources.

organize to arrange in an orderly way:

> If you *organize* your ideas, the speech you give will be much clearer and more persuasive.

gather to bring together in one place or group:

> The students will *gather* information from the Internet.

matter *n.* anything that has weight and takes up space:

> *Matter* can be a solid, a liquid, or a gas.

material what something is made of:

> This window is made from an unbreakable *material*.

substance a material that has certain qualities:

> Ink is a *substance* that can make a stain.

mass a shapeless body of matter:

> A *mass* of mud flowed down the mountainside.

mean *adj.* not nice:

> The *mean* characters had no friends at the end of the story.

cruel actively mean:

> No one should be *cruel* to animals.

unkind harsh, without kindness:

> Cinderella's stepsisters were *unkind* to her.

heartless uncaring:

> The villain in the story was cold and *heartless*.

meant *v.* past tense and past participle of mean. had in mind:

I *meant* to write that letter today.

intended set about with a purpose:

Reba *intended* to become a scientist.

planned thought out ahead of time:

Dr. Reyes *planned* to see six patients that morning.

designed made for a special use or purpose:

That seat was *designed* for a small child.

aimed tried to reach a goal:

I *aimed* to be the best writer I could be.

middle *adj.* the same distance from either end:

I sat in the *middle* seat in the row.

halfway the same distance between two places or two ends:

The cowboy reached the *halfway* point of his ride.

central at or near the middle:

We'll hold the meeting in a *central* spot that is easy for everyone to reach.

---

mighty *adj.* having or showing great power, strength, or ability.

brawny	powerful
forceful	strong
hardy	superhuman
invincible	tough
muscular	unyielding
potent	

■ antonyms: weak, feeble, frail

---

mild *adj.* not extreme:
> She prefers food with a *mild* taste, but he likes spicy dishes.

soothing able to ease irritation:
> The cream was *soothing* on his chapped skin.

bland without any harsh or extreme qualities:
> *Bland* foods include rice and cottage cheese.

calm quiet:
> The ocean is *calm,* and the wind is still.

mission *n.* a special job:
> The astronauts trained for their *mission* to the space station.

assignment a specific task that is given out:
> Each student was given an *assignment* to complete during vacation.

duty something that a person is supposed to do:
> It's the teacher's *duty* to explain the fire drill procedure.

mistake *n.* something that is not correctly done:
> I corrected the *mistake* I made on the test.

error something that is wrong:
> The students found only one spelling *error* in their article.

blunder a careless or stupid mistake:
> It was a serious *blunder* to forget the time of the game.

fault a weakness or mistake:
> The lack of light was a *fault* in the design of the workroom.

mistaken *adj.* formed from the past participle
of the verb mistake. based on error:
  Ilya had the *mistaken* belief that the game
  began at noon.
misinformed in error because of false or
wrong information:
  Harry's *misinformed* ideas about
  computers are a result of
  ignorance.
incorrect not correct or right:
  A lot of people have *incorrect* notions
  about healthful eating.

---

modern *adj.* having to do with the
present day or with recent times.

contemporary	present
current	recent
fresh	up-to-date
new	up-to-the-
novel	minute

■ antonyms: old, old-fashioned, antique,
antiquated, out-of-date, outdated, obsolete

---

moist *adj.* containing some water:
  The ground still feels *moist* after
  yesterday's rain.
damp a little wet:
  Use a *damp* sponge to wipe up spills.
wet containing or covered with water:
  The car's hood was *wet* with rain.

nap *v.* to sleep for a short time:
I like to *nap* in the shade on a hot summer afternoon.

doze to sleep lightly or for a short time:
A cat can *doze* for a few minutes and wake up full of energy.

snooze to sleep for a short time:
The puppies play for a while and then *snooze* on the rug.

rest to lie quietly but not necessarily to sleep:
Robbie will *rest* on his bed for an hour before the game starts.

narrow *adj.* having only a small amount of space between one side and the other:
The deer jumped easily over the *narrow* stream.

thin not thick, having little space between one side and the other:
I was full, so I only took a *thin* slice of cake.

slender not big around:
The *slender* snake slipped into the tiny gap between the rocks.

slim not thick; skinny:
The *slim* boy was just able to squeeze between the two stacks of boxes in the crowded storeroom.

natural *adj.* to be expected:
It is *natural* to be excited about winning a contest.

normal logical or natural:
Stage fright is a *normal* reaction for actors to have.

typical usual, to be expected:

Running around noisily is *typical* behavior for young children.

nature *n.* of a specific type:

I like books of a scientific *nature*.

category a class into which like things can be grouped:

Swimming belongs in the *category* of water sports.

sort a type or category:

That's not the *sort* of sweater that I like to wear.

kind a type or category:

What *kind* of fruit do you like best?

variety a different kind or form:

Have you tried the new *variety* of cheese?

naughty *adj.* behaving badly:

Sneaking cookies can be a *naughty* thing to do.

disobedient refusing or failing to carry out someone's wishes or orders:

The baby-sitter said not to climb on the table, but the *disobedient* child did it anyway.

mischievous playful in a way that causes harm or trouble:

That *mischievous* puppy is chewing on my slipper again.

near *prep.* a short distance from:

The library is *near* the museum.

close to not far from:

I live *close to* school.

beside right next to:

Roger usually stands *beside* Paco in the student chorus.

against touching:

Ugo leaned the folding chair *against* the wall.

nearby *adj.* not far away:

My best friend lives in a *nearby* house.

neighboring next to or near:

He drives to work in a *neighboring* town.

bordering right next to:

The *bordering* states for Florida are Georgia and Alabama.

neighborhood *n.* a small area where people live:

We moved to a *neighborhood* that has no apartment buildings.

community a group of people who live in the same place:

My *community* voted to build a new town hall.

block the length of a street in a town or city:

All the houses on my *block* have red front doors.

---

noise *n.* a loud or harsh sound.

bang	**clang**	**jingle**
blast	**clank**	**pop**
buzz	**din**	**racket**
blare	**hiss**	**roar**
boom	**jangle**	**sound**

■antonyms: silence, quiet

---

note *v.* to put something in writing:
> Graciela will *note* the address in her phone book.

jot to write something quickly or in few words:
> I took a minute to *jot* down my idea for the story.

record to write something down so as to keep an accurate memory of it:
> Choose one group member to *record* your discussion.

scribble to write quickly and often messily:
> I can't read your writing when you *scribble*.

nothing *n.* not anything:
> Ten minus ten leaves *nothing*.

zero nothing:
> If none of your answers on the test are correct, your score will be *zero*.

none no one or not one:
> Six people started the puzzle, but *none* finished it.

notice *v.* to become aware of:
> The teacher will *notice* if we put in extra effort.

observe to look at with attention:
> *Observe* the scene carefully so you can remember the details later.

mark to give attention to:
> *Mark* my words; you'll be sorry if you don't.

heed pay attention to:
> The child did not *heed* the warning and fell on the slippery ice.

notion *n.* a thought that something might
be true:

Mariko had the *notion* that the movie
would end happily.

theory a supposition that is based on some
evidence but is not proved:

Len's *theory* is that the book's characters
are based on real people.

assumption something that is taken for
granted to be true:

Our *assumption* was that you wanted to
eat with us.

nourish *v.* to provide food or other substances
that promote health and growth:

The honey in one beehive can *nourish*
thousands of bees.

sustain to supply with nourishment:

Freeze-dried foods are easy to pack and
can *sustain* hikers for many days.

feed to provide food or nourishment:

This powdered formula is designed to *feed*
babies.

novel *n.* a long work of narrative writing,
usually fiction:

The author published his first *novel* when
he was fifty years old.

book a long work of fiction or nonfiction:

I just read a wonderful *book* by Yoshiko
Uchida.

story a long or short narrative work, usually
fiction:

The last *story* I read took place in
Australia.

tale a story, usually fictional, that can be short or long:

This adventure *tale* kept me reading until late at night.

obey *v.* to carry out wishes, orders, or instructions:

Most drivers *obey* the traffic laws.

follow to act according to wishes, orders, or instructions:

If you *follow* the directions, you'll do it right.

comply to act in agreement with a rule or request:

The people who *comply* with the order to form a line will be dismissed first.

odd *adj.* not ordinary or expected:

The story had an *odd* ending that took us by surprise.

unusual not ordinary:

The bus driver took an *unusual* route to school today.

strange unfamiliar, a little mysterious:

The animals in the desert made *strange* sounds.

offer *v.* to present for acceptance or rejection:

If you are hungry, I can *offer* you a peanut butter sandwich.

suggest to mention as a possiblility:

I *suggest* we go to the movies today.

propose to put forward a plan:

We *propose* to write an outline before we write the report.

official *adj.* coming from or permitted by a proper authority:
These are the *official* T-shirts worn by athletes for City Sports Week.
approved permitted by the proper authority:
In our apartment we must use only an *approved* air conditioner that doesn't overload the wiring.
authorized officially approved:
The *authorized* life story of my favorite TV star will be published next spring.

often *adv.* many times:
I *often* have toast for breakfast.
frequently many times:
Mrs. Garcia *frequently* calls on the students in the back row.
usually most of the time:
It *usually* gets warmer this time of the year.
repeatedly again and again:
During pitching practice, Mike threw the ball *repeatedly*.

oily *adj.* Covered or soaked with oil:
The puddle had an *oily* film on it.
greasy coated with grease, oil, or other fat:
Engine parts are often *greasy,* so handle them carefully.
slimy covered or coated with a thin, sticky film:
People think that snakes are *slimy,* but their scales are dry and smooth.

open *adj.* not having its lid, door, or other covering closed:

It was easy to see the toys in the *open* toy chest.

uncovered not having the lid or cover on:

Steam rose from the *uncovered* soup pot cooking on the stove.

unclosed not having its door or other covering shut:

An *unclosed* box will allow dust to get inside.

opinion *n.* a conclusion based on judgment and feelings as well as facts:

It is my *opinion* that everyone should have the chance to take music lessons.

belief an opinion:

I hold the *belief* that anyone can become a good athlete.

conviction a firm belief or opinion:

It is Danny's *conviction* that people will do the right thing if they are treated right.

view a particular way of looking at something; an opinion:

What is your *view* on the way our state's environment is being protected?

order *v.* to tell someone to do something:

The coach will *order* the team to do push-ups.

command to order:

The police officer used a loud voice to *command* drivers to turn right.

instruct to give an order:

The leader will *instruct* the group to stop at the end of the road.

force to make someone do something:
No one can *force* you to tell a lie.

ought *v.* to have a duty or to be expected to:
Prentiss *ought* to help Connie wash the dishes.
should another word expressing duty:
I *should* do my homework before I play.
must another word expressing duty, but stronger than ought or should:
To ride this bus, you *must* pay with exact change.

outfit *n.* a set of clothes:
I got a new *outfit* for my birthday.
clothing things worn to cover the body:
He had on too much *clothing* for such a hot day.
ensemble a coordinated outfit or costume:
A bright green cap matched the shirt and pants and completed the eye-catching *ensemble*.
attire set of clothes:
The actors changed into street *attire* before leaving the theater.

outside *n.* the outer part:
The *outside* of the house was painted green.
covering anything that covers or is outside:
The box had a *covering* of velvet.
skin the outer covering of a person or of some kinds of animals:
A snake's *skin* is dry and cool.
shell a hard outer covering:
To eat a peanut, you have to take off its *shell*.

exterior the outside:

The *exterior* of the house was dark red brick.

overcome *v.* to beat:

Can our players *overcome* a more skillful team?

defeat to win against or beat:

This year, our city's swimmers will *defeat* everyone else.

outdo to do better than:

I hope to *outdo* the other runners in the race.

surpass to do better than:

I can *surpass* the grades I got last year.

overlook *v.* to fail to see:

Don't *overlook* the article I told you about.

neglect to fail to do:

Don't *neglect* to study your notes.

miss to fail to notice, find, or catch:

I didn't *miss* any errors in punctuation.

skip to pass by or leave out:

Did you *skip* the third question by accident?

own *v.* to have or hold as a belonging:

I *own* a purple notebook.

have to hold as a belonging:

They *have* a house on River Street.

possess to own:

Mr. and Mrs. Gomez *possess* a two-car garage.

keep to have from now on:

I will get to *keep* the gold cup I won as a prize.

package *n.* one or more objects that are wrapped or boxed:

I received a large *package* on my birthday.

parcel one or more objects that are wrapped up, usually to be mailed:

I sent him a *parcel* of candy and fruit.

bundle a group of things wrapped or tied together for ease in carrying:

Gerry carried the *bundle* of laundry to the cleaners.

patches *v.* present tense of patch. sews a piece of cloth over a hole or a tear:

Ariana *patches* the jeans.

mends fixes:

Hal *mends* the rip in his shirt.

darns repairs clothing by sewing up a hole or a tear:

Gil *darns* the hole in his sock so he doesn't have to throw the pair away.

repairs fixes:

Jan *repairs* the broken lamp.

path *n.* a trail or way made for walking:

We walked up the *path* that leads to the river.

trail a way, usually narrow, made for walking:

The hikers traveled single file along the *trail*.

route a traveled way:

The map showed an old trade *route*
through Asia.

road a way made for walking or for vehicles:
The unpaved *road* gave cars a bumpy ride.

street a way in a city or town that is usually
paved, and is often bordered by sidewalks:
Wait for the green light before crossing
the *street*.

pedestrian *adj.* lacking originality,
imagination, or excitement:
Farida thinks that this author has a
pedestrian style of writing.

commonplace not original or remarkable:
This picture seems *commonplace* to me
because it looks like dozens of others
I've seen.

dull not interesting:
Your stories won't be *dull* if you set them
in some of the unusual places you have
visited.

peer *v.* to look hard or closely so as to see
something clearly:
I tried to *peer* through the grime on the
window to see who was inside.

look to use one's eyes, to see:
Look at the pictures and choose the one
that you like best.

gaze to look long and unusually attentively at:
They stopped to *gaze* at the toys displayed
in the window.

stare to look very hard at:
Their aunt told them it was rude to *stare*
at people.

perfect *adj.* without flaw or error in its appearance or nature:

A *perfect* math test is one with no mistakes.

faultless without error—often describing performance or behavior:

The gymnast performed a *faultless* routine with no mistakes.

flawless without imperfections such as marks or bumps:

The marble's smooth surface was *flawless*.

ideal exactly what is hoped for or needed:

Blue is the *ideal* color for these walls.

perfume *n.* a sweet or pleasant smell, usually of flowers or the like:

The delicate *perfume* of roses filled the room.

fragrance a sweet or delicate smell—usually of flowers, pine trees, other plants, spices, and similar smells:

Lilacs keep their *fragrance* even after they are cut from the bush.

aroma an agreeable smell—used more broadly than perfume:

The *aroma* from the steaming soup pot made Graciela's mouth water.

scent a smell, often an agreeable or delicate one:

The breeze held the *scent* of the ocean.

odor any smell, good or bad:

Eli detected the *odor* of detergent on the freshly washed towel.

permit *v.* to give someone leave to do something:

> Our city does not *permit* people to park their cars on downtown streets.

allow to give permission:

> Does the arena's management *allow* people to take pictures while the game is going on?

let to allow:

> *Let* me help you move that sofa.

person *n.* a man, a woman, or a child:

> There was one *person* standing in line when the ticket booth opened.

human a person and not an animal:

> You can see from the shape that these footprints were made by a *human*.

individual one single person:

> The first *individual* to answer this question will win the prize.

pier *n.* a structure built out over the water used as a landing place for boats and ships:

> There are always adults and children fishing off the end of the *pier*.

wharf a structure built along a shore as a landing place for boats and ships:

> The merchant's house was close to the *wharf* where his ships unloaded.

dock a platform where boats and ships are tied up:

> We crossed the gangplank from the *dock* to the deck of the ship.

plain *adj.* not fancy:
> The woman drove a *plain* car even though she was rich.

simple without anything added:
> Nat made a *simple* cake with no icing.

ordinary regular, not special:
> The queen had on an *ordinary* dress without any decoration.

everyday ordinary, not fancy:
> We wore our *everyday* clothes to the party instead of dressing up.

dull plain in a boring way:
> This room looks *dull* because it has no pictures on the walls.

plate *n.* a shallow, flat container from which food is eaten:
> Put some mashed potatoes on each person's *plate*.

dish a plate or shallow bowl used for eating:
> This *dish* is the right size for dessert.

platter a large, shallow dish used for serving food:
> Pass the *platter* of meat around to everyone at the table.

saucer a small plate made for holding a cup:
> She rested the cup on the *saucer*.

pleasant *adj.* giving a good feeling:
> The mountain views make this walk *pleasant*.

enjoyable easy to find satisfying:
> Swimming on a warm day is *enjoyable*.

agreeable likable:
> She has an *agreeable* personality.

delightful highly pleasing:

An icy glass of water is *delightful* on a hot, humid day.

power *n.* strength:

Do you have enough *power* to open this jar?

force the power to move or stop something: The *force* of the wind blew down several trees.

energy strength or eagerness to do things: Children can play all day without running out of *energy*.

ability the strength or skill to do something: Cats have the *ability* to jump up to high places.

---

practical *adj.* having the possibility of being used or carried out; making sense.

functional	**serviceable**
realistic	**sound**
reasonable	**usable**
sensible	**workable**

■ antonyms: impractical, unrealistic, unworkable

---

prehistoric *adj.* belonging to a time before people started writing history:

Woolly mammoths lived in *prehistoric* times but do not exist today.

primitive of or having to do with an early or original state:

The archaeologist found pieces of *primitive* pottery.

ancient of or having to do with times very long ago:

The ring of stones was the only sign of an *ancient* fort on top of the hill behind the farm.

prevent *v.* to keep something from happening or someone from doing something:

The barricade was meant to *prevent* people from falling in the hole.

stop to keep something from moving or acting:

They tried to *stop* the skateboard from rolling into the storm drain.

hinder to hold back:

Don't let me *hinder* you from catching your bus.

thwart to prevent someone or something from succeeding:

The hero tried to *thwart* the plans of the evil king.

pride *n.* an exaggerated sense of one's own worth or importance:

Rod's *pride* keeps him from seeing that other people might know more than he does.

conceit a very high opinion of oneself or one's achievements:

The singer was filled with *conceit* after he won three talent contests.

vanity too much concern with one's looks, abilities, deeds, or the like:

That movie star is famous for her *vanity* and is always being photographed in a different outfit.

prize *n.* something that is won in a contest or game:

> The winner of the game got a silver ring as a *prize*.

trophy a cup, small statue, or other object given as a prize:

> After the final game, our team got a *trophy* in the shape of a baseball glove.

medal a coin-shaped metal piece given as a prize:

> The winner of the race will get a gold *medal*.

award something that is given for excellence:

> He won an *award* in the contest.

promise *n.* a guarantee given that one will or will not do something:

> My mother made a *promise* to be at all of our team's softball games.

assurance a declaration or guarantee:

> Mr. Fong gave his *assurance* that the repair would be finished by Friday.

word a promise:

> Maria always keeps her *word* when she says she'll do something.

pledge a formal promise:

> I made a *pledge* to my parents to keep my room tidy and my bed made.

protest *n.* an objection against something:

> The letter was written as a *protest* against the new rules.

objection an expression of not liking or approving:

> They made an *objection* to the mayor about the plan to close the library.

complaint a statement that something is wrong:

> The toy company took our *complaint* seriously.

provide *v.* to give what is needed or wanted:

> One cup of cottage cheese will *provide* a high amount of protein and calcium.

supply to give something needed or wanted:

> Each family will *supply* room and board for an exchange student.

furnish to supply or provide:

> The cafeteria will *furnish* all the meals for the weekend activities.

deliver to carry or take to a destination:

> The entertainment company says it can *deliver* everything we need for our graduation party.

offer to present to be accepted or turned down:

> That bus company claims to *offer* the lowest fares.

---

prowl *v.* to move or roam quietly or secretly.

creep	skulk
glide	sneak
lurk	steal
slink	

- antonyms: barge, strut, swagger, clump, parade, march, stride

---

purpose *n.* why something is done:

> The book's *purpose* is to inform us.

reason why something happens or is done—more of an explanation than an aim:

What is your *reason* for being late?

intention aim:

Our *intention* is to wash all the windows.

goal aim:

Winning is Thea's *goal*.

quality *n.* something that makes a person or thing what it is:

Patience is a *quality* that athletes need as they train.

feature an important part or quality of something or someone:

Dependability is a *feature* of all the machines our company makes.

trait a feature or quality:

Jana's most obvious *trait* is her creativity.

characteristic a feature:

A strong beat is a *characteristic* of danceable music.

quantity *n.* a number or amount, often large:

A vast *quantity* of food is always left over at our family dinners.

profusion a plentiful amount:

A *profusion* of papers covered Andy's desk.

abundance a quantity that is more than enough:

Because Gerry always has an *abundance* of ideas for stories, her worst problem is deciding which idea to write about.

quarrel *n.* an angry disagreement:
  The neighbors had a *quarrel* about
  parking spaces.
  argument a discussion of something by
  people who do not agree:
    It is possible for people to have an
    argument without getting angry.
  conflict a strong disagreement:
    The two groups tried to resolve their
    conflict peacefully.
  squabble a dispute or argument over
  something small and unimportant:
    Two of my uncles are always having a
    squabble about who gets to choose the TV
    channel.

question *n.* a matter to be talked over:
  We discussed the *question* of sports clubs.
  problem a matter needing to be solved:
    The meeting will deal with the *problem*
    of noise.
  issue a matter to be thought about, not
  necessarily a problem:
    Recycling is an *issue* that many people
    have opinions about.
  topic a subject or matter to be examined:
    What would make a good *topic* for a
    speech to parents?

quick *adj.* having speed:
  The cat made a *quick* movement with its
  paw and caught the fly.
  fast having speed:
    My sister is a *fast* runner and wins many
    races.
  speedy quick:

We worked at a *speedy* pace.
rapid quick:
Many birds have a *rapid* heartbeat.

quickly *adv.* at a high speed or in a short time:
I went *quickly* to my mother and told her what happened.
rapidly with great speed:
The marbles rolled away *rapidly*.
speedily quickly:
The waiter went *speedily* from table to table.
fast at high speed or in a short time:
The fan cooled the room *fast*.

---

quiet *adj.* making little or no noise.

hushed	soundless
muffled	speechless
muted	still
noiseless	unspeaking
silent	whispery

- antonyms: noisy, loud, blaring, booming

---

quietly *adv.* with little or no noise:
Cats walk *quietly* on their padded paws.
soundlessly without noise:
The hands of my electric clock move *soundlessly* across its face.
silently with no noise:
The snake moved *silently* across the sand.
stealthily sneakily, so as not to be noticed:
He tiptoed *stealthily* toward the refrigerator.

quit *v.* to stop doing something.

cease	pause
conclude	rest
end	shut down
finish	stop
halt	wind up

- antonyms: begin, start, go, continue

quite *adv.* completely, fully:
I have not *quite* finished writing.
completely in total, all:
The barrel is *completely* full.
entirely completely, all:
It will be *entirely* your fault if you are late.
wholly completely, in total:
The company is *wholly* owned by one
family.

racket *n.* a loud or confusing noise

blast	reverberation
clamor	roar
clatter	stir
din	tumult
hullabaloo	uproar
pandemonium	

raise *v.* to pick up or move to a higher place:
　Raise your hand if you have any questions.
lift to pick up:
　Can they *lift* the table by themselves?
boost to push or shove up:
　Give me a *boost* so I can reach the
　window ledge.
heave to lift, raise, pull, or throw, usually with
effort:
　The farm workers will *heave* the crates of
　carrots onto the truck.

rapidly *adv.* with great speed:
　A hummingbird's heart beats much more
　rapidly than a human's heart.
quickly fast:
　The chef sliced the vegetables so *quickly*
　that her hand movements were almost a
　blur.
speedily rapidly:
　The clock's second hand turned *speedily*
　as I rushed to finish the test before the
　bell rang.
swiftly with great speed:
　In a 100-meter dash, the runners move so
　swiftly that the race seems to end as soon
　as it begins.
hastily quickly, often urgently or carelessly:
　Lee gathered his papers up *hastily* and
　stuffed them into his bookbag.

reach *v.* to come to:
　We will *reach* the hotel by sunset.
arrive to get to or come to:
　When you *arrive* at the museum, wait for
　me in the front hall.

land to come to the ground or to shore:

The plane should *land* at the airport soon.

approach to come near:

The ships slow down as they *approach* the dock.

ready *adj.* Set for use or action:

The soup is heated up and *ready* to eat.

prepared made ready:

The gym has been decorated and *prepared* for the dance.

ripe fully grown, in a condition to be eaten:

We'll eat these *ripe* pears for lunch.

ready-made *adj.* made in quantity and not to order:

Long ago, people sewed their own clothes, but now most of us buy *ready-made* clothes.

mass-produced made in large quantities, usually by machine:

Mass-produced toys don't have the beauty or personality of handmade ones.

manufactured made by machines, especially on a large scale:

Hand-carved chairs take longer to make than *manufactured* ones.

really *adv.* in fact:

That actor looks like a child, but he is *really* eighteen years old.

actually really:

Is the moon *actually* made of cheese?

indeed in fact:

Silk thread is *indeed* made by silkworms.

absolutely without a doubt:

This is *absolutely* my favorite story.

recall *v.* to bring back to mind:

   I know we've met, but I can't *recall* your name.

   remember to bring an image or idea from the past to mind:

   Do you *remember* the words to the song?

   recollect to bring something back to mind:

   After exchanging news, the old friends began to *recollect* the adventures of their childhood.

receive *v.* to take or get:

   I hope to *receive* a letter from my pen pal soon.

   accept to take something that is given:

   Our neighbor asked us to *accept* the gift with her thanks.

   acquire to get or gain as one's own:

   They hope to *acquire* more books for the library.

   get to come to have or own:

   That swimmer will *get* a ribbon at the end of the race.

   obtain to get through effort:

   They wrote to the director to *obtain* permission to visit the Space Center.

remain *v.* not to go away:

   I washed the shirt many times, but the stains and splotches *remain.*

   stay not to leave:

   Will you leave the party early or *stay* until it ends?

   last to go on:

   We were sure our friendship would *last* forever.

endure to remain:
Even after all these years, the friendships I made in kindergarten *endure*.

continue to keep on happening, being, or doing:
The festival will *continue* for three more days.

reply *v.* to answer in words or writing:
Did you *reply* to her letter?

answer to say or write something in return:
Will you *answer* his question right away?

respond to say or write something in return:
Think about how you will *respond* to the question.

retort to give a quick, witty, or sharp answer:
If you ask her that, she will probably *retort* jokingly.

require *v.* to order or compel:
My teachers *require* me to have neat handwriting.

demand to require as necessary or useful:
This film will *demand* your full attention so that you don't miss any clues.

insist upon to demand firmly and strongly:
Our coaches *insist upon* our attendance at each practice.

expect to consider as necessary or right:
Once you join this club, we *expect* you to volunteer an hour each week for community service.

respect *v.* to feel or show a high regard for:
My friends *respect* someone who always tells the truth.

esteem to consider good or important:
I *esteem* your opinion of my writing, so
I'm glad you like this story.

value to prize:
People *value* Carlos's advice because he
thinks carefully before giving it.

admire to feel high regard for:
I *admire* people who can stay calm in an
emergency.

return *v.* to come or go back:
The visitor promised to *return* soon.

recur to happen or appear again:
The pain in my knee might *recur* if I don't
let it heal.

revisit to come to the same place again:
They plan to *revisit* the place where they
first played together.

river *n.* a large body of flowing water that
empties into a lake, ocean, or other river:
That *river* is deep enough for ships to
travel on.

stream a body of flowing water, usually
smaller than a river:
The *stream* ran through the woods.

creek a small body of flowing water:
The water in the *creek* was too cold to
wade in.

waterway a river, canal, or other body of
water used as a route for ships:
The Mississippi River is an important
waterway.

roam *v.* to go around, especially over a large area, without any purpose or destination:

> When the family tours a new city, Dad decides on his route beforehand, but Mom likes to *roam* around with no special plan.

ramble to go about aimlessly:

> Early evening is a nice time to *ramble* through a museum.

rove to wander aimlessly from place to place:

> The campers *rove* around the field, examining the plants and wildflowers.

meander to wander here and there:

> The tourists *meander* through the downtown shopping area.

roar *v.* to speak or make sounds in a loud, deep voice:

> If she hits a home run, the crowd will *roar.*

bellow to make a loud sound or speak very loudly:

> Why does he *bellow* if I'm standing right here?

shout to call loudly:

> The announcer had to *shout* to be heard over the cheering audience.

scream to make a sudden, sharp, loud cry:

> This fake giant spider made my brother *scream.*

yell to give a loud cry, or to speak loudly:

> I heard him *yell,* "We won!"

rock *n.* a piece of naturally hard material from the earth:

> I gave my brother a *rock* for his collection.

stone a rock, or the material that a rock is made from:

> The wall was made of pieces of gray *stone*.

pebble a tiny rock:

> A *pebble* was stuck in my shoe.

boulder a large rock:

> That *boulder* is as tall as an adult person.

rough *adj.* not smooth:

> Greg used sandpaper on the *rough* wood.

coarse made of large grains or threads instead of fine, smooth ones:

> Burlap is a *coarse* cloth, while satin is a fine one.

bumpy covered with lumps:

> The clay pot had a *bumpy* surface.

jagged with sharp or broken edges:

> That *jagged* piece of glass could cut your hand.

row *n.* a group of people or things arranged one next to the other:

> She placed her toys in a neat *row* on the shelf.

line a number of people or things arranged one after the other:

> A long *line* of people waited to get into the theater.

column a long row or line:

> The band marched in a straight *column* down the street.

rush *v.* to move or go quickly:

He had to *rush* toward the ball in order to catch it.

hurry to move faster than usual:

Let us *hurry* across the street before the light turns red.

dart to move suddenly and quickly:

The cats *dart* across the room to chase the fly.

dash to move fast:

The children *dash* after the runaway dog.

speed to move quickly—used for vehicles as well as living things:

The cars *speed* along the highway.

scare *v.* to make afraid:

Sudden movements can *scare* the dog.

frighten to make afraid:

That movie didn't *frighten* me—much!

alarm to disturb or make afraid:

The prediction of tornadoes should *alarm* people living in that area.

startle to frighten or take by surprise, usually not seriously:

Did that boom *startle* you?

terrify to frighten greatly:

A lion's roar can *terrify* zebras.

scarlet *adj.* a bright red or orange-red color:

Mimi's *scarlet* coat was a bright contrast to the dreary gray sky.

red the color of objects such as stoplights,

blood, and many fire engines:
> The flashing *red* lights alerted us to the ambulance's approach.

crimson a deep red:
> Some people think that *crimson* lipstick is very elegant.

ruby a deep red, like the jewel of the same name:
> Betty's *ruby* velvet dress made her stand out in the crowd.

scatter *v.* to spread or throw about here and there:
> If you *scatter* birdseed, the birds won't have to crowd together to eat it.

strew to spread or throw about at random:
> The flower girls *strew* rose petals in the bride's path.

disperse to break up and send off in different directions:
> Put the leaves in a bag, or the wind will *disperse* them and we'll have to rake again.

disseminate to scatter things or ideas widely:
> Volunteers will *disseminate* these leaflets throughout the city.

---

scream *v.* to make a loud cry.

bellow	roar	whoop
crow	screech	yell
cry	shout	
howl	shriek	

■ antonyms: whisper, squeak, murmur

secret *adj.* kept from others or shared with only a few.

concealed	mysterious
covered	undercover
disguised	unknown
hidden	veiled
masked	withheld

■ antonyms: open, revealed, known

section *n.* a part of a whole:
> After the game, Yuki ate an orange *section* as a snack.

portion a part of a larger whole:
> Everyone received a *portion* of the profits from the sale at the street fair.

segment any of the parts into which an object may be divided:
> Each *segment* of the apple should be the same size.

slice a thin, flat piece cut from a larger object:
> Doug cut a *slice* of pizza.

severe *adj.* very strict or harsh:
> The punishment for the crime was *severe*.

strict following or enforcing rules in a careful, exact way:
> He was known as a *strict* teacher.

stern serious and strict:
> At first he seemed *stern*, but later we realized how kind he was.

grim stern, frightening, and harsh:
> They feared to go before the *grim* judge.

sew *v.* to use needle and thread to make or repair clothes:

Sasha will *sew* a vest to wear to the party.

stitch to sew:

I will *stitch* those buttons onto your coat.

mend to use needle and thread to repair clothes:

Lee needs to *mend* the hem of that dress.

darn to mend by making stitches back and forth across a hole or rip:

Ms. Ritts wants to *darn* the hole in her daughter's sock.

shadows *Noun,* pl. of shadow. dark areas made when rays of light are blocked by a person, animal, or thing:

You will feel cooler if you walk in the *shadows* cast by the buildings.

shade a place sheltered from the sun:

Sit in the *shade* of this tree.

dimness an area of very little light:

In the *dimness,* the table was hard to see.

darkness an area with little or no light:

I heard footsteps, but in the *darkness,* I saw no one.

shear *v.* to cut with scissors or clippers:

We watched the farmer *shear* the wool from the sheep.

clip to cut:

The barber can *clip* just a little off your hair to make it even.

prune to cut off or cut out parts, usually of plants:

They *prune* the new growth from the vines each autumn.

trim to cut away or remove parts to make something neat:

I *trim* the edges of each article before putting it in the scrapbook.

crop to cut or bite off the top part of something:

They keep the goat in the yard to *crop* the grass.

---

shelter *v.* to provide cover or protection for.

cover   safeguard
enclose   screen
guard   shield
hide   surround
protect

- antonyms: display, uncover

---

signal *n.* something used to warn, direct, inform, or instruct:

The coach used a hand *signal* to let us know where to throw the ball.

sign an action or hand movement used as communication:

Corazon waved her hand as a *sign* that she had seen Mickey.

gesture a movement of the head, body, or limbs to express or communicate something:

Peg's shrug was a *gesture* that showed her confusion.

motion the act of moving the body or one of its parts:

Mr. Park used an arm *motion* instead of words to get the chorus to sing more loudly.

silent *adj.* making no sound:
One dog barked loudly, but the other was *silent*.
soundless making no sound:
In my sneakers, I have a *soundless* walk even if I don't tiptoe.
noiseless not making noise:
Some machines hum, click, or buzz, but others are *noiseless*.
quiet making little or no noise:
The audience was *quiet* except for a few coughs and rustles.

slippery *adj.* having a surface so smooth that it can cause one to slide or fall:
Walk carefully on that *slippery* ice.
smooth having an even or polished surface:
Smooth ice is best for skating.
slick smooth, usually because of a film like ice or oil:
Spilled oil made the floor *slick*.
glassy with a surface like glass:
The ice storm made the road *glassy*.
icy covered with ice:
Icy roads can be dangerous to drive on.

smart *adj.* quick at learning:
John is a *smart* student.
bright very smart:
Terry is *bright,* but she also studies hard.
intelligent knowing a lot:
Every *intelligent* person should know some history.

wise not only smart but also using good judgment:

A *wise* person thinks before speaking.

song *n.* a piece of music that also has words:

We heard a beautiful *song* on the radio.

tune a set of musical notes that can be sung or whistled:

Can you whistle this *tune?*

melody a series of musical notes:

That *melody* sounds familiar.

sort *v.* to separate according to kind or size:

We were told to *sort* the clothes by color.

classify to arrange in groups:

The instructor told us to *classify* the animals by what they ate.

categorize to group or classify things:

The librarian said to *categorize* the magazines by topic.

file to put away in an arranged order:

His job was to *file* the papers in alphabetical order.

---

special *adj.* different from others in a certain way; not ordinary.

choice	**rare**
distinguished	**remarkable**
exceptional	**superior**
extraordinary	**uncommon**
noteworthy	**unique**
outstanding	

■ antonyms: ordinary, common, usual, unremarkable

---

strange *adj.* not known before now:
> A *strange* boy stood at the door of Jan's old house.

unfamiliar not heard of or seen before:
> An *unfamiliar* girl was talking to my sister.

unknown unfamiliar:
> The voice on the phone was *unknown* to me.

strength *n.* the quality of being strong:
> They weren't sure they had the *strength* to move the file cabinet.

energy the strength or eagerness to work or do things:
> We always have more *energy* early in the morning.

power the ability to do something:
> My sister has the *power* to throw a ball all the way across the gym.

vigor active power or force:
> The neighborhood group opposed the plan for a new mall with *vigor*.

force the power to move or stop something:
> The *force* of a tornado's winds can lift a car into the air.

strong *adj.* able to lift or move things easily:
> Furniture movers are very *strong*.

powerful able to do something or bring something about:
> This car's *powerful* engine lets it go very fast.

tough able to put up with hardship:
> Settlers had to be *tough* to travel all the way across the country in covered wagons.

subject *n.* something thought, written, or talked about:

> What was the *subject* of the visitor's lecture?

topic what a speech, discussion, or piece of writing is about:

> The *topic* of the article should appear in the first paragraph.

problem a question to be thought about and answered:

> We eagerly tackled the *problem* of how to organize the art supplies.

issue a subject that is being discussed or considered:

> They felt that the central *issue* was who would get to go on the trip.

sudden *adj.* happening quickly and without warning:

> The *sudden* bang from the car's engine made me jump.

startling surprising, happening without warning:

> The outcome of the elections was *startling* to all of us.

unexpected coming without warning, but not necessarily sudden:

> An *unexpected* storm flooded the streets.

unpredicted not guessed or expected ahead of time:

> The team's win had *unpredicted* results.

quick fast:

> The *quick* movement of the cat's paw surprised the squirrel.

tale *n.* a story:

> Have you heard the *tale* of the fisherman and his wife?

story an account of something that happens:

> I wrote a *story* about a mysterious horse.

fable a story that teaches a lesson:

> In that *fable,* the steady tortoise beats the fast hare.

legend an old story that may not be entirely true:

> Do you know the *legend* of Robin Hood?

tall *adj.* having more than average height:

> That tree is so *tall* that it reaches above the roof of the house.

lofty reaching high into the air:

> The *lofty* mountaintops seemed to pierce the clouds.

towering very tall:

> The streets were lined with *towering* oak trees.

sizable somewhat large or tall:

> A *sizable* flagpole stood in the center of the yard.

tardy *adj.* arriving or happening after the appointed time:

> She left early, but she was still *tardy.*

late coming after the usual time:

> Our uncle was *late,* so we started lunch without him.

overdue delayed beyond the appointed time:

> Their books were *overdue* and the fine was ten cents a day.

taught *v.* past tense and past participle of teach. helped someone learn:

Mr. Chan *taught* me how to use a hammer.

instructed taught:

Celia *instructed* the class in how to use the new computers.

showed helped someone learn by explaining how to do something:

I *showed* my little sister how to read a book.

explained made clear:

My parents *explained* what to do in case of a fire.

tease *v.* to annoy or make fun of in a playful way:

It's not a good idea to *tease* a porcupine.

annoy to bother or disturb:

Will it *annoy* you if I turn on the radio?

ridicule to make fun of:

The shortstop feared that his teammates would *ridicule* him for dropping the ball.

mimic to imitate, especially in order to make fun of:

I promised not to *mimic* my little brother any more.

taunt to challenge or insult:

The fans sometimes *taunt* the referee.

terrible *adj.* very bad or unpleasant:

We had *terrible* weather on our vacation.

horrible very bad, ugly, or unpleasant:

The garbage gave off a *horrible* smell.

unbearable difficult or impossible to stand:

The piercing sound was *unbearable* to listen to.

awful very bad:

Those colors look *awful* together.

threat *n.* a person or thing that is a source of injury or harm:

Air pollution is a *threat* to people's health.

danger a person or thing that is a source of harm, injury, or loss:

An ice storm can be a *danger* to drivers who try to drive too fast.

menace a person or thing that is a harm:

A wild dog on the loose can be a *menace* to children.

throw *v.* to send through the air:

Throw the ball over here.

toss to throw a short distance:

Toss me that glove, will you?

pitch to throw or toss:

She can *pitch* a baseball very well.

fling to throw carelessly:

Please don't *fling* your clothes all over the room.

told *v.* past tense of tell. put into words:

Sam *told* wonderful stories.

said put into words:

Al *said* I could borrow his new book.

spoke used words, talked:

Roger *spoke* about the new animal park.

explained used words to make clear:

Jess *explained* how to bake muffins.

tough *adj.* difficult:

Cleaning this floor is a *tough* job.

hard not easy:

Our teacher gave us a *hard* math problem for extra credit.

troublesome causing trouble or difficulty:
Getting puppies to behave can be a
troublesome job.

uphill against difficulties, as if going up a hill:
Training a cat can be an *uphill* task.

travel *v.* to go from place to place:
We will *travel* by airplane to England.

journey to travel:
The explorer planned to *journey* to the
North Pole.

voyage to travel by water or through space:
The astronauts will *voyage* to the moon.

roam to travel with no particular place in
mind:
I left home to *roam* around the United
States.

tremble *v.* to shake as with cold, weakness,
fear, or anger:
As I lifted my cat onto the vet's examining
table, I felt her entire body *tremble*.

shake to move quickly to and fro, up and
down, or from side to side:
I tried to keep my voice firm as I
addressed the audience, but I was so
nervous I could feel my knees *shake*.

shiver to shake, as with cold or fear:
The swimmers *shiver* as they get out of
the pool.

quiver to shake slightly, often with fear or
excitement:
The children seemed to *quiver* with
excitement, as though they couldn't hold
still.

trophy *n.* a cup, small statue, or other prize given to someone for winning a contest or doing something outstanding:

Jack won a *trophy* for making the best chili.

prize something that is won in a contest or game:

The *prize* for winning the race was a blue ribbon.

award something that is given for merit or excellence:

The fifth grade class won an *award* for their mural.

medal a flat coin-shaped piece of metal, often attached to a ribbon, usually given as a reward for an achievement:

Each member of the winning Olympic softball team received a gold *medal*.

cup an ornament in the shape of a cup, offered as a prize:

The team members' names were engraved on the *cup* that they won.

trouble *n.* worry or difficulty:

He had *trouble* learning the computer program.

problem difficulty:

I have a *problem* doing this dance step.

worry an uneasy or fearful feeling:

My *worry* is that it just won't work.

twin *adj.* being identical or very much alike:

In the science fiction story, the planet had *twin* moons.

matching being similar or equal to another:

The singer and the drummer wore
matching costumes.

identical exactly alike:

The *identical* cars were parked side by
side.

twirl *v.* to turn rapidly:

When tops *twirl,* their colors seem to flow
together.

spin to turn quickly:

If I twirl this coin, it will *spin* so fast that
its flat shape will blur into a sphere.

whirl to spin:

The pinwheel's blades *whirl* in the wind.

type *n.* a group of things that are alike or have
the same qualities:

What *type* of animal would you like as a
pet?

kind a group of things that are the same in
some way:

There is only one *kind* of paper on the
shelf.

sort a group of people or things that have
something in common:

They were the *sort* of people who always
make you feel welcome.

class a related group of people or things:

Mammals are one *class* of animals, and
reptiles are another.

category a group or class of things:

We had to choose a *category* for each
spelling word.

uncertain *adj.* not known for sure:
  The outcome of the election is still
  uncertain because all the votes haven't
  been counted.
  doubtful not clear or sure:
  Megan's plans for tomorrow are *doubtful*
  because she still doesn't feel well.
  undecided not agreed upon:
  The outcome of the competition will
  remain *undecided* until the judges finish
  reviewing the entries.
  unsettled not agreed upon:
  The family's vacation plans are still
  unsettled because no one can agree on
  either choice.

understand *v.* to get the meaning of:
  Did you *understand* the math?
  grasp to see or get the meaning of:
  Can you *grasp* the sense of this poem?
  follow to pay attention to and understand:
  His story was hard to *follow.*
  know to understand clearly or be sure of:
  I *know* how to add and subtract numbers.
  learn to get to know:
  To *learn* sewing, watch someone who
  knows how.

uneven *adj.* not smooth or flat:
  The sidewalk's surface was so *uneven* that
  the children couldn't skate on it.
  rough not smooth or level:

The tree's bark was *rough* and scratchy.

bumpy full of bumps, not smooth:
The car bounced along on the *bumpy* road.

irregular not even or uniformly shaped:
The moon has an *irregular* surface that is full of craters.

unfair *adj.* not fair, right, or just:
The election was *unfair* because some votes were not counted.

unjust not right, not deserved:
It is *unjust* to punish us all for what one person did.

wrong not right, not to be allowed:
Letting someone get away with cheating is *wrong*.

unequal not well matched; unfair:
When the older children played the younger children in football, it was an *unequal* contest.

unhappy *adj.* not happy:
I am always *unhappy* when my favorite team loses.

sad unhappy:
The movie had a very *sad* ending.

gloomy in a sad mood:
It's easy to feel *gloomy* on a dark, rainy day.

miserable very unhappy:
When our dog was very sick, we were *miserable*.

union *n.* something formed by joining two or more people or units for a common purpose:

> Several countries formed an economic *union* that had special trade agreements for members.

federation a union formed by agreement between states, nations, or other groups:

> Many countries joined the new business *federation*.

association a group of people or organizations that get together for a purpose:

> Local artists formed an *association* to promote their work.

unknown *adj.* not known, not heard of or seen before now:

> That man is *unknown* to me.

unfamiliar not heard of or seen before:

> An *unfamiliar* voice was speaking.

strange not known before now:

> A *strange* girl is sitting in Pete's old seat.

mysterious puzzling or hard to explain:

> My mother investigated a *mysterious* scratching noise and found a lost kitten outside our door.

unnecessary *adj.* not needed or useful:

> This car is full of *unnecessary* features that add to its price without improving its quality.

needless unnecessary:

> If you don't make a plan beforehand, you will waste your energy and time doing *needless* tasks.

useless serving no purpose:
   The important-looking knobs on that
   machine are *useless* and are there just for
   decoration.
superfluous more than is needed or wanted:
   Many toys are sold in showy display boxes
   that use a lot of *superfluous* packaging
   materials.

upset *n.* an unexpected result in a contest,
competition, or election:
   The mayor lost the election in an *upset.*
defeat a loss in a contest or competition:
   The team had faced *defeat* before.
thrashing a severe defeat or loss, often
unexpected:
   The sportscaster announced that the
   home team took a *thrashing* in the final
   game of the series.

urgent *adj.* calling for immediate action or
attention:
   The leaking sink pipe is an *urgent* matter
   that the plumber should know about now.
pressing requiring action or attention right
away:
   Rescue workers in that town have a
   pressing need for blankets and canned
   food.
compelling driving; urgent:
   The shortage of classroom space is a
   compelling problem that must be dealt
   with at once.
critical at a point of crisis:
   A high fever in a child is a *critical*
   situation that needs a doctor's attention.

useful *adj.* having a good use or purpose:
A first aid kit is a *useful* thing to have on
a trip.

helpful giving help:
The people at the store offered *helpful*
information.

valuable having great use or importance:
Baby-sitting has been a *valuable*
experience.

beneficial having a good effect:
A vacation will be *beneficial* to our
health.

usual *adj.* done or used by habit:
We took the *usual* route to Grandma's
house.

regular usual, routine:
This is not my *regular* desk.

ordinary common or normal:
It was an *ordinary* box with no
decoration.

everyday not special:
We used our *everyday* dishes even though
it was a party.

vacant *adj.* containing nothing or no one:
After the movers left with the family's
furniture, Imelda took a last look at the
vacant rooms.

empty having nothing or no one inside:
The carton was so light that Greg knew it
was *empty*.

unoccupied containing no one, unused:
There was only one *unoccupied* seat on the benches in the crowded waiting room.
abandoned once used but now left behind:
The *abandoned* shed was falling to ruins.

vacation *n.* time off away from school or work:
Are you going away during your *vacation?*
holidays time off away from school or work:
He spent his summer *holidays* in Canada.
recess a time when school or work stops:
Spring *recess* begins next week.

van *n.* a kind of truck:
The moving *van* carried our furniture to our new home.
truck a vehicle used to carry loads, not passengers:
The *truck* carried vegetables from the farm to the supermarket.
pickup a small truck with an open back:
Mr. Lang filled his *pickup* with bricks and concrete and drove to the building site.

vanish *v.* to cease to exist:
When you press this button, whatever is on your computer screen will *vanish* if you don't save it first.
disappear to vanish:
When I scrub hard, the stains on the floor will *disappear* completely.
evaporate to vanish:
Her fears always *evaporate* as soon as she turns on a light.

fade to disappear gradually:
> The sound of the radio will *fade* as the batteries grow weaker.

variety *n.* a number or collection of different things:
> The store sells a *variety* of greeting cards.

assortment a collection of different things:
> A bowl on the table held an *assortment* of fruits.

array a large, impressive collection of things:
> The *array* of shoes in my mother's closet could stock an entire shoestore.

hodgepodge a disorderly collection of things:
> The drawer held a *hodgepodge* of writing tools.

---

vary *v.* to be or become different.

adjust	modify
alter	shift
change	transform
fluctuate	

---

vault *n.* a room or compartment that is safe for keeping valuables:
> Be sure to put all the documents in the hotel *vault* as soon as you get there.

safe a strong metal box or other container used to store money, jewelry, and other valuables:
> The *safe* was built into the wall and hidden behind a picture.

safe-deposit box a metal box for storing valuables inside a bank vault:
    After each of their children was born, Mr. and Mrs. Swenson put the birth certificate in the family's *safe-deposit box*.

venture *n.* an attempted project or task that involves some risk or danger:
    Don't take part in a risky business *venture* unless you can afford to lose the money.
enterprise an attempted project or task, especially a difficult or important one:
    Sending astronauts to Mars is an *enterprise* that could have great benefits for humankind.
undertaking something that is tried or worked on:
    Learning to speak a second language is a difficult but worthwhile *undertaking*.

verse *n.* words written in a particular rhythmic pattern and often in rhyme:
    Martha designs birthday cards and writes a *verse* in each one.
poetry words chosen and arranged to create a feeling and meaning through sound and rhythm:
    The program consisted of *poetry* and music.
rhyme verse or poetry having sounds at the ends of lines that are alike or the same:
    Mattie wrote a funny *rhyme* that the town newspaper printed.

village *n.* a community made up of a small group of houses:

The *village* didn't even have a main street.

town community that is larger than a village:

Our *town* has an elementary school and a high school.

city a large community where many people live and work:

A *city* can have thousands or even millions of people.

visitor *n.* a person who visits:

That woman is a *visitor* to our class for the day.

guest someone who has been invited to visit:

We are having a *guest* to dinner tonight.

caller someone who comes to your home for business or friendship:

The *caller* rang the doorbell.

voyage *n.* a long trip:

The family went on a *voyage* to Mexico.

journey a trip, usually long:

The *journey* took him through India.

cruise a trip by water:

The ocean *cruise* took three days.

trip travel that can be long or short:

Let's take a *trip* to the shore.

tour a trip with several stops, perhaps to look at the sights:

A *tour* of the West might include a stop at the Grand Canyon.

waste *n.* things that are thrown away:
The *waste* from some kitchens after a party could feed an entire family.
rubbish useless things:
I cleaned the *rubbish* out of the attic.
garbage food and other things that are thrown out:
Twice a week the truck comes by to pick up the *garbage*.
trash unwanted things that are thrown away:
Put the *trash* in the can under the sink.
scrap worn or used material that can be used again in some way:
We used the *scrap* from the sewing class to make a quilt.

---

weak *adj.* not having strength.

usually said of people or animals:	usually said of things:
delicate	**flimsy**
feeble	**shaky**
frail	**tumbledown**
sickly	**unsteady**

■ antonyms: strong, powerful, healthy, muscular, sturdy, solid

wealth *n.* a great amount of money or valuable things:

People with great *wealth* can often buy things to make their lives more comfortable.

riches a great amount of money or valuable things:

The museum displayed the *riches* from the king's palaces.

money coins and bills in general, or wealth:

His family always had *money*.

property land, buildings, or other materials that are owned:

In his will, he left some of his *property* to charity.

weary *adj.* having little or no energy:

They felt *weary* after the long walk.

tired drained of energy:

After a hard day's work, I am too *tired* to stay up late.

exhausted very tired, completely drained of energy:

Jane was *exhausted* after painting the house all day.

worn-out very tired:

Chasing after a young child all day left me *worn-out*.

sleepy needing to go to sleep:

I start feeling *sleepy* around 9:00 p.m.

whine *v.* to cry in a soft, high complaining voice:

They heard the puppy *whine* from behind the closed door.

wail to make a mournful cry:

The cats always *wail* when they're hungry or want attention.

whimper to cry with weak, broken sounds: The child might *whimper* in fear when the dog begins to bark.

whirl *v.* to turn quickly in a circle or around a central point:
   The dancers *whirl* so fast that their faces are a blur.

spin to turn quickly in a circle or around a central point:
   A pinwheel's blades *spin* when I blow on them.

rotate to turn, slowly or quickly, around a central point:
   The wheels of a car *rotate* on axles, making the car move.

---

wind *n.* air that is moving over the earth.

breeze	**gale**
blast	**gust**
cyclone	**squall**
draft	**tornado**

---

wonder *v.* to want to know or learn:
   I *wonder* why fog forms.

suppose to think about what something could be like:
   Suppose you have ten dollars to spend and must choose something to spend it on.

imagine to picture a person or thing in one's mind:
   Can you *imagine* what it would be like to be an acrobat?

wonderful *adj.* very good; fine.

delightful	pleasant
enjoyable	pleasing
exciting	pleasurable
fascinating	refreshing
favorable	satisfying
gratifying	splendid
joyful	terrific
marvelous	

■ antonyms: unpleasant, disagreeable

world *n.* the earth:

The explorer Sir Francis Drake traveled all around the *world* on a sailing ship.

planet a heavenly body that circles a sun.

Our world is a *planet,* and so is Mars.

Earth the name of our planet:

The planets closest to *Earth* are Venus and Mars.

globe the world:

Astronauts flying in space can circle the *globe* in just a few hours.

worn *Adjective,* formed from the past participle of the verb *wear.* damaged by use or wear:

I put on my *worn* jeans when I work in the garden.

shabby worn out and faded:

The musician's coat was *shabby* but clean and neatly patched.

frayed separated into loose threads:

Fold the *frayed* hem of the skirt under and sew it down.

threadbare worn out so much that the threads show through:

My favorite shirt is too *threadbare* to wear to school.

ragged worn out and torn:

A *ragged* shirt was all we found in the abandoned house.

worry *v.* to cause to feel uneasy:

The motor's scraping noises *worry* me.

distress to cause to feel anxious or upset:

Newspaper reports can *distress* us.

concern to cause to feel interested, often in an uneasy way:

Even a low fever can *concern* a parent.

bother to cause to feel annoyed:

A dripping faucet can really *bother* me.

worthy *adj.* Having worth or value:

Is this book *worthy* of a good review?

deserving worthy of:

The principal will give the scholarship to a *deserving* student.

worthwhile having enough value or importance to be worth the time or effort:

Music is a *worthwhile* activity as well as an enjoyable one because it sharpens math and memory skills.

valuable of great use, worth, or importance:

Typing is a *valuable* skill because these days everyone uses computers.

write *v.* to form letters, words, or numbers on paper or another surface:

Lu likes to *write* with a ballpoint pen.

print to write in separate letters like the letters in books:

Ahmed tried to *print* his name neatly.

scribble to write quickly or carelessly:

If you *scribble* that phone number too quickly, you won't be able to read it.

input to enter information into a computer:

Ellen will *input* her story and print it out.

wrong *adj.* not correct:

Most of your answers were right, but some were *wrong*.

incorrect wrong:

If you believe that whales are a kind of fish, you are *incorrect*.

untrue not a fact:

It is *untrue* that all people with brown hair have brown eyes.

yarn *n.* a continuous strand of wool or other fiber, used to knit or weave:

He knitted the *yarn* into a vest.

string a thin strand of fibers used for tying:

Use *string* to attach the discs to the mobile.

twine a stronger, thicker string:

He tied the boxes together with *twine*.

cord a continuous strand that can be made of fiber but doesn't have to be:

The lamp has an electric *cord* and a plug.

rope a thick, strong cord:

The boat was attached to the dock with a *rope*.

thread a very thin strand of fiber used in sewing:

I used red *thread* to sew on that button.